Labor Law

A Basic Guide to the National Labor Relations Act

David E. Strecker

CRC Press
Taylor & Francis Group
Boca Raton   London   New York

CRC Press is an imprint of the
Taylor & Francis Group, an **informa** business

This book, Labor Law: A Basic Guide to the National Labor Relations Act, is designed for employers, students, and others interested in labor law. The information presented should prove extremely useful in understanding the issues raised and their legal context. This book is not, however, a substitute for experienced legal counsel and does not provide legal advice or attempt to address the numerous factual issues which invariably arise during any employment-related dispute. Although we have attempted to cover the major developments in the National Labor Relations Act, this book is not all-inclusive, and the current status of any decision or principle of law should be verified by counsel.

CRC Press
Taylor & Francis Group
6000 Broken Sound Parkway NW, Suite 300
Boca Raton, FL 33487-2742

© 2011 by Taylor and Francis Group, LLC
CRC Press is an imprint of Taylor & Francis Group, an Informa business

No claim to original U.S. Government works

Printed in the United States of America on acid-free paper
10 9 8 7 6 5 4 3 2 1

International Standard Book Number: 978-1-4398-5594-2 (Hardback)

Library of Congress Cataloging-in-Publication Data

Strecker, David E.
   Labor law : a basic guide to the National Labor Relations Act / author, David E. Strecker.
        p. cm.
   Includes bibliographical references and index.
   ISBN 978-1-4398-5594-2
   1. Labor laws and legislation--United States. 2. Collective bargaining--Law and legislation--United States. 3. Labor unions--Law and legislation--United States. I. Title.

   KF3369.S77 2011
   344.7301--dc22
                                                                                          2010036241

Visit the Taylor & Francis Web site at
http://www.taylorandfrancis.com

and the CRC Press Web site at
http://www.crcpress.com

Labor Law

A Basic Guide to the National Labor Relations Act

For Katherine

Contents

About the Author

David E. Strecker, JD, has been practicing labor and employment law for over thirty years. He is admitted to practice in New York and Oklahoma and represents clients from all sectors of industry and business. His legal experience encompasses the full range of employment law, including labor relations, employment discrimination, wrongful termination, workplace safety, wage/hour matters, policy/handbook preparation, employment contracts, noncompete covenants, and employee benefits. He is an experienced advocate before state and federal courts and administrative agencies.

Strecker is a regular speaker at Continuing Legal Education (CLE) seminars and has published several articles on labor and employment law issues. He teaches labor relations at Oklahoma State University in Stillwater, Oklahoma and negotiation and management skills at the University of Tulsa in Tulsa, Oklahoma. Strecker graduated from Cornell University in Ithaca, New York with a Juris Doctorate (cum laude) and a master's degree in Industrial and Labor Relations. He received his undergraduate degree (magna cum laude) from Westminster College in Fulton, Missouri. He is a member of the American Bar Association and the Oklahoma Bar Association. He is also a member of the Society for Human Resource Management. His name appears in *The Best Lawyers in America* and *Who's Who in America*. He is a lieutenant colonel (retired) in the U.S. Army Judge Advocate Generals Corps.

Preface

This book is about labor law. Whether you are a supervisor, a business owner, or a student, *Labor Law: A Basic Guide to the National Labor Relations Act* will help you understand one of the most important aspects of the workplace: the laws and rules governing how one treats employees. In particular, the area of labor law is crucial to understand. It is often counter-intuitive. Your common sense will not always provide the right answer.

To many, labor law is a difficult subject: intimidating to some and misunderstood by others. The goal of this book is to give you a solid, basic understanding of this area of the law. It will not make you an expert, but it will educate you enough to let you manage with the confidence that comes from knowing the rights and obligations of employees, the company, and supervisors.

Labor and employment law has assumed an increasingly important role in our society. New laws, such as the Family and Medical Leave Act, the Americans with Disabilities Act, and various state enactments, create new rights and problems. Older laws, such as the Fair Labor Standards Act, have been recently amended or been supplemented by new regulations. Court cases constantly expand or limit the scope of the laws and attempt to define ambiguous parts of these laws. The trend of employment law in the past sixty-five years has generally been to give employees greater rights and limit those of the employers. Gone are the days when the boss could fire an employee and have absolutely no fear of a lawsuit.

Yet, employers still enjoy tremendous power over the workplace, unlike in some other industrialized nations. The author firmly believes, after over thirty years of practicing in this field, that employers usually can accomplish most of their employee relations goals lawfully, and successfully manage this aspect of their business more or less as they would like. The key to this is making labor and employment laws work for you rather than viewing it as an obstacle.

With the resurgence of labor unions, this often neglected subject of manager education deserves to be studied anew. Unions have developed new tools of organizing and are prepared to expand to industries and workers not heretofore targeted by labor. Unions have become sophisticated and, quite frankly, have a lot to offer employees in many—although certainly not all—situations. Some studies show that almost 60 percent of American workers want a union to represent them, but are fearful of confrontations with management if they take action to organize.

Although most of my experience has been representing management in this area, I have had the opportunity to develop some different perspectives. I have worked in factories, retail stores, and other employments. I have been a union member. I have worked in a human resources department of a large employer who had employees represented by unions, and I have a master's degree in labor relations as well as a law degree. Both in my military and civilian careers, I have been a supervisor myself. I have seen the workplace from almost every angle. I believe I can help you understand labor law.

In *Labor Law: A Basic Guide to the National Labor Relations Act*, "labor law" will be used to designate those laws governing the relationship between a company and unions. "Employment law" will generally refer to everything else, such as discrimination laws, wage/hour laws, safety laws, etc. This book deals only with private sector labor law arising under the National Labor Relations Act. It does not deal with public sector labor law or the Railway Labor Act.

This book is primarily an introduction to labor law. Nevertheless, we will discuss some aspects of employment law and also give a brief introduction to the legal system itself.

Chapter 1

Introduction to Labor and Employment Law

The Importance of Labor and Employment Law in Our Society

Once upon a time, the owners of a business were like gods in the sense that they had total authority over all that took place within the confines of their establishments. Employees were no exception to this rule, and they often suffered at the hands of supervisors who were insensitive, if not outright hostile, to the needs and feelings of their subordinates. Hours of work, pay, safety, time off, and other terms and conditions of employment were dictated by the company. Employees could be discriminated against or refused employment altogether because of sex, race, religion, or age. Any employee who was a union member (or thought to be) would be terminated. Job classifications and lines of promotion were often segregated by race or sex. Safety rules and protective equipment were virtually unheard of and many employees suffered horrible injuries or death with little or no compensation to them or their families. Most employers had absolutely no sympathy for an employee's family obligations and time off was a rare commodity. There were no human resource departments and no employee assistance programs. Employees who complained about any of the above could be fired at will.

Things are different now. Largely as the result of the abuses summarized above, today's employers are confronted with a vast quilt-work of laws regulating how they treat their employees.

Probably the two most important sets of laws are (1) those dealing with discrimination in the workplace and (2) those dealing with labor union–management relations. Antidiscrimination laws have opened up workplace opportunities and resulted in a more diverse workforce.

Labor relations laws have contributed to industrial peace and largely freed our economy from crippling strikes and labor turmoil. A lot of people complain about these laws, claiming they interfere with a company's right to run its business as it pleases. It is widely recognized, however, that these laws have done our society a lot of good. They are not going away. Regardless of how you feel about these and other employment laws, it is best to learn them—and learn to live with them.

From an employee's viewpoint, many of the workplace laws that exist today are taken for granted. All employees expect, for instance, that they will receive time and one half their regular rate for hours worked in excess of forty per week. The right to join a union, although controversial in some quarters, is largely accepted and taken as a given. The right to apply for a job regardless of the color of your skin is now well entrenched in our society. These and other rights have come to be an integral part of the fabric of society. You, as a supervisor, should not expect to be commended for complying with these laws or applauded by your employees. Compliance is expected. This is how central labor and employment law have become in our society.

Think of how the workplace would operate (or would not operate) if these laws were not in place. Initially, you might say that it would be a good thing: that you would not be shackled with regulations and rules. On the other hand, consider what kind of workplace we would have if employees could be trampled on at leisure or where personal bias and prejudice could run rampant. You might not be in the job you are in now if such were the case.

Think also of how many deserving, talented people might not get to demonstrate their talents because of their sex or skin color. Consider, from the employer's point of view, how many good employees would not be able to advance (or never would have been hired) and thus deprive the employer of their talent and energy.

Think of how you could run your department, plant, or business if your employees could walk out on strike any time they wanted to do so. What if labor unions could deny members even the most basic of rights to elect officers or approve dues?

The upshot of all of this is that labor and employment law (along with other laws) help our economy run smoothly. If you do not believe me, look at the labor turmoil seen in other countries in the past few years that do not have a similar legal system.

In sum, by regulating the workplace and those in it, labor and employment law helps our economy function and, in turn, this helps our society and its members enjoy the fruits of our labors.

The Importance of Labor and Employment Law in Running a Business

Most people look at labor and employment laws (or any laws for that matter) as impediments to running a business. To some extent, this is true. Nevertheless, much of what the law requires us to do is to treat people fairly. Most supervisors want to do this anyway. It is in the nature of most people to be fair (or to think they are being fair).

In my years of practice, however, I have not encountered a law that prevents a business from being run in an efficient manner. To be sure, sometimes we must accommodate the law in our business planning, but we should not confuse this with inefficiency. If we correctly factor the law into our planning operations, the company will be money ahead. Why do I say this? Because the law will not go away. If we operate in ignorance or in defiance of it, we will eventually lose. This may take the form of lawsuits, administrative charges, fines, low morale, high turnover, low productivity, or a combination of the above.

Employees are a crucial component of any business and good employee relations are necessary to obtain and retain good people. Recruiting, hiring, pay systems, bonuses, corrective action, benefits, safety, discharge, and other employment actions must be planned and attended to just as carefully as marketing or production. The law is intertwined with all employment actions. For instance, discrimination laws influence how we advertise for openings, interview the applicants, and make the hiring decisions. Wage/hour laws govern whether we pay people for on-call time or when we must pay overtime. Workplace safety rules may affect how we build an addition to the facility or the placement of machinery.

If we try to do any of the above things without taking the law into account, trouble of one type or another is bound to result. On the other hand, if our planning and execution are consistent with legal requirements, we can do pretty much what we want. But first, you must have a good working knowledge of the law.

Aims of This Book

This book is about labor law, one of the oldest and, arguably, the most important of all workplace laws. The main purpose of this book is to explain the basics of labor law in simple terms. Beyond this, however, it is my aim to show you how to work with our labor laws and to view them as an aid, rather than as an obstacle, to accomplishing your goals as a supervisor.

After finishing this book, hopefully, you will understand:

■ How labor unions come into the workplace.
■ What a company can and cannot do under the law when a union is organizing its workforce.

- What are unfair labor practices and how to avoid them.
- What terms are commonly found in labor contracts and what they mean.
- How to prepare for labor negotiations.
- How labor contracts are negotiated.
- The duty to bargain in good faith; what it means.
- Common features of grievance and arbitration procedures.
- The legal status of labor arbitration and how to prepare a case for an arbitration hearing.
- Various forms of strikes and their legal basis.
- Unlawful work stoppages.
- Employer lockouts.

While this book will not make you a labor law expert, it will give you a good framework to use in spotting what may be problem issues and formulating a solution. You also will be more confident in dealing with employee issues once you know what laws govern your actions. Finally, you will understand that the basics of these laws are not hard to learn or apply. While complicated situations may call for expert advice, you will at least be able to know when to "call in the cavalry."

An Explanation of Some Terms and the Basics of the Legal System

I have already explained how the terms "labor law" and "employment law" will be used in this book. It will be useful to understand some additional terms and the basic workings of the legal system.

The Structure of the Law and Its Nature and Sources

A **law** is a rule or set of rules that govern our behavior. There are usually penalties for violating a law; these are sometimes referred to as the "Teeth of the Law." There are two basic places where we go to find laws: **statutes** and **court decisions**. Statutes are laws enacted by a legislative body. This could be the United States Congress or your state legislature. This also might include the laws enacted by the governing body of a city or town, such as a city council. Instead of being called "statutes," however, such laws are usually referred to as **ordinances**.

Constitutions are found at both the federal and state level. Constitutions are a type of statute because they usually are created by a legislative body of some sort. Of course, we all learned in school how the U.S. Constitution came into being as the result of the efforts of our Founding Fathers. States also have constitutions usually created by the state legislature, special conventions, or territorial legislatures at about the time the state was admitted to the union. Constitutions are different from normal legislation in two respects. First, they are usually more basic than legislation in that they deal with such issues as the fundamental rights of citizens, the structure of government, and the electoral process. Second, they are more difficult to amend or repeal than a normal statute. Usually, to amend a constitution it takes more than a majority vote of the legislature or perhaps even a vote of the people (or the states in the case of the U.S. Constitution).

In modern times, some laws create **administrative agencies** to enforce them. Administrative agencies play an important role in many areas of labor and employment law. A primary example in the area of labor law is the National Labor Relations Board, created by Congress to enforce the National Labor Relations Act. Other examples of this would be the Equal Employment Opportunity Commission created by Congress to enforce the Civil Rights Act of 1964, and the Occupational Safety and Health Administration (OSHA) which regulates workplace safety. State administrative agencies may be created by a state legislature to enforce laws it enacts. An example of this might be a state agency created to enforce a state's labor laws, wage-hour laws, or antidiscrimination laws.

The **regulations** created by an administrative agency are not strictly law, but often have the force of law. In other words, we had better follow them unless we can show that the agency went beyond what it was supposed to do, that is, it exceeded the power given to it by the legislative body that created it. For our purposes, however, we will assume that regulations must be followed. If they are to be challenged, the decision will be made by your company's legal counsel. It is important to know that courts will give great weight to an agency's rules and its interpretation of those rules.

As we shall see, in the case of the National Labor Relations Board, many of its "rules" are hammered out in case decisions as opposed to detailed regulations. This fact sets the Board apart somewhat from other administrative agencies. To be sure, the Board has its regulations but, by and large, it governs procedure as opposed to substantive issues.

Laws can be created by courts as well. This is known as **common law** or **judge made law**. Sometimes courts create law when there is not a statute covering the area. At other times, courts interpret vague or unclear provisions of statutes and such interpretations become a part of the law. It is difficult to summarize common law because one has to read a lot of court cases to get the "big picture." One of the main common law rules we will discuss in this book is the federal common law exceptions governing the legal status of labor arbitration.

Civil and Criminal Law

The law also can be looked at in at least two other ways. First is whether the law is civil or criminal. Civil law pertains to rules, which, if broken, the violators are "punished" by (1) monetary penalties often referred to as **damages** and (2) orders of a court to comply with the law in the future (these orders are known as **injunctions**). Criminal law also lays down rules. If these rules are broken, however, the wrongdoer is subject to imprisonment as well as monetary penalties, often called **fines**.

Some laws are both civil and criminal. A good example of this would be federal laws dealing with securities fraud. Someone who breaks these rules could be liable to be sued in civil court or prosecuted in criminal court (or both), depending on which rule or rules he or she broke. Most laws governing the workplace are civil in nature.

Civil Law

Civil law is usually enforced through law suits. These lawsuits are filed by individuals or companies (or organizations) against the person or company they claim violated their rights. Trials are often conducted in front of a jury, which will make a decision once all the evidence has been presented to them. Sometimes a jury verdict does not have to be unanimous, depending on the state involved and the size of the jury. The person bringing the lawsuit is known as the **plaintiff** and the person defending is the **defendant**. The plaintiff has the burden of proof. In other words, he or she must prove the case by a "preponderance of the evidence." This means that the plaintiffs must show their claims are more than likely true. If the evidence is evenly balanced, the plaintiff loses because he or she has failed to carry the burden of proof. It is important in the labor and employment law area to know that administrative agencies can sometimes bring a civil suit against an employer for a violation of the laws they administer.

Criminal Law

Criminal law is enforced through law enforcement personnel (police, etc.) and through the district attorney, county prosecutor, or similar official. Criminal trials are often conducted with a jury. The government has the burden of proof to prove guilt "beyond a reasonable doubt." Usually, the jury verdict must be unanimous. This burden of proof is much higher than the "preponderance of evidence" standard used in civil trials.

When Laws Conflict

We can also look at the law as a "pecking order." Because of the **supremacy clause** in the U.S. Constitution, federal law will always be at the top of the pecking order. In other words, if a federal law and state law conflict, the federal law will control. For instance, some state laws say women are not allowed to work in certain occupations. Federal law, however, says that women can work in *any* occupation. In this instance, federal law "trumps" state law. It works the same way if a state law and city ordinance conflict. The state law will always control.

This "pecking order"(often called *preemption*) is important in labor law. It is because of this that federal labor laws will usually control in the case of any conflict with state law or whenever a state tries to regulate private sector labor management relations. As with most legal rules, however, there are exceptions. For instance, if a state law gives a *worker* greater rights than federal law, then state law may apply. Even then, however, it is *federal law* that dictates which law will govern.

Also, a constitution will always win over a statute or a court decision. You have probably heard of a court decision that holds a law to be "unconstitutional." This means the court decided that there was a conflict between the constitution and the law. If a law is in conflict with a constitution, the constitution always trumps.

The Judicial System

Court systems differ widely from state to state. Some generalities hold true, however, in almost all states. One of these is that there is a "pecking order" in the judicial system. The **trial court** is the lowest court in the pecking order of courts. This is the court that conducts the jury trial whether it is civil or criminal. Some states have separate criminal courts, but most states provide for only one court system to try both civil and criminal cases at the trial court level.

Next, there is the **intermediate appellate court**. Sometimes it is called the *court of appeals*. It hears cases that are appealed by the losing party at the trial court level. The party who does not like the decision of this court may appeal it to the highest state court, usually called the **state supreme court**. Further appeal is usually not available unless federal issues are raised allowing an appeal into the federal system.

Appellate courts do not usually hear witnesses or hold hearings where evidence is introduced. They decide cases on a "paper record" of what happened in the trial court and on the basis of **briefs** submitted by the parties. A brief is a written argument as to why a party should win the appeal. Sometimes an appellate court will allow the parties to present an oral argument in front of the court, in addition to submitting briefs.

In the federal system, the upward pecking order is as follows: **United States District Court**, **Circuit Courts of Appeal**, and the **United States Supreme Court**. A United States district court will have jurisdiction over cases that arise in a geographical area known as the **district**. An example would be the United States District Court for the Northern District of New York. Courts of appeal are organized around a geographic area known as a **circuit**. The circuit is usually comprised of all the district courts in a group of several states. An example of this would be the United States Court of Appeals for the Tenth Circuit, which includes the district courts in the states of Utah, Oklahoma, Colorado, Kansas, New Mexico, Wyoming, and Montana.

The federal circuit courts are important in the labor law arena because, if a party wants to appeal a decision of the National Labor Relations Board, such appeals are usually lodged with such courts.

Some states have special appeals courts to hear particular kinds of cases. For instance, some states have an appellate court dealing only with criminal cases. Other states have a special court dealing with appeals in the Workers Compensation System.

The rulings and decisions of both federal and state administrative agencies can usually be reviewed by courts within the judicial system. For instance, a decision and order of the National Labor Relations Board can be reviewed by a federal circuit court of appeal.

The Fundamentals of Tort Law

A **tort** is defined as *a wrong done to another person*. Beyond this, a tort is *a wrong for which the law will provide a remedy*. A tort is a civil wrong, and not criminal in nature. Some torts also may be crimes. For instance, assault is both a civil wrong and a criminal violation in most states. Other torts, such as negligence, are usually civil only. Torts may be either intentional torts or negligence-based torts.

Intentional Torts

Intentional torts include assault, battery, causing another person severe emotional distress, conversion (taking another's property), slander, libel, or false imprisonment. The key element here is that the actor intends to commit the act in question. He or she may not intend the precise harm caused by the act, but, nevertheless, will be liable for all harm caused. For instance, "I become angry at a co-worker and hit him, thinking only to teach him a lesson for insulting me. My blow is harder than I thought it would be. His skull is fractured and he is disabled for life. Even though I did not intend to cause such severe harm, I will be liable for it because I did intend to commit the tort of battery."

An **assault** is an act that puts another in reasonable fear of bodily harm. If I come at you with a baseball bat and start to swing it, I have assaulted you. If I throw a stapler at you and miss, I have committed an assault.

A **battery** is an unlawful act of physical touching. A blow, a push, a shove, hitting someone with an object, are all batteries.

False imprisonment consists of an unjustifiable confinement of another person, either literally (as in locking someone in a room) or through threats of harm to them or to others, for example, telling an employee he/she cannot leave a room until he/she has confessed to stealing from the company. It is important to understand the concept of intentional torts when studying labor law. For instance, strikers who commit such torts while on the picket line may lose statutory protections they would otherwise have. If union officials are involved, it could rise to unfair labor practice charges. State court injunctions are often sought to stop such conduct.

In some cases, the law allows us to do harm to another. **Self defense** or **defense of another** are the two main examples of this. If you reasonably fear that someone is about to do harm to you or to another person, you are allowed to use whatever force is necessary to prevent the harm. In most states, deadly force may only be used, if necessary, in self defense (or defense of another) to prevent death or serious bodily injury. In some states, if you can remove yourself from danger, you must attempt to do this before defending yourself. This is known as the **duty to retreat**. Other states do not recognize this principle, but only require that you reasonably perceive you are in danger of being harmed. In those states, you may defend yourself even if you could retreat.

Negligence—Before you can be sued for a tort based on negligence, there must be a **duty** on your part either to act or refrain from acting. If you have no duty, then you cannot be liable. For instance, assume I am walking down the street and see two strangers fighting each other. It appears that one is gaining the advantage and is about to seriously injure the other. I do nothing and he or she is seriously harmed. Am I liable because I should have done something to stop the violence? The answer is "no." You may say that I had a moral obligation to stop the violence and you might be correct. But I had no legal obligation to break up the fight because I had no duty under the law to do so.

If, however, you do have a duty to another person, then you must act reasonably and can be held liable for any harm done to that person caused by your negligence. When does one person owe a duty to another? A good example will be a parent's duty to his or her child. Another example is a duty owed by those who operate public transportation (such as a bus driver) to their passengers. School personnel also may have a duty to protect students and the school system may owe a duty to its employees as well. Most importantly, employers have a duty to provide their employees a safe workplace. They also have a duty to protect others who are lawfully on their property, such as contractors, vendors, and suppliers.

Negligence can consist of either taking action or a failure to act. If I drive my car at night without lights and have a wreck because no one can see me, I have committed a negligent act. I will be liable for any harm this act causes to others. If I am the driver of a city bus and notice a passenger is having what appears to be a heart attack and I do nothing, I have failed to act in a situation where I had a duty to act. Once again, this is considered to be negligence and I may be liable to the passenger.

For me to be liable to pay damages, the negligence must be the proximate cause of the harm. In other words, my negligent act must have directly led to the damage. If I cause a car accident by running into the rear of another car, I am certainly liable for the damage to the other car and to those injured in the crash. However, if the driver of the car I hit is wanted by the police, and he runs away from the scene and is hit by another car, I am not liable for his injuries because they were not directly caused by my negligence. Proximate cause is often measured in terms of what would be the reasonably foreseeable results of the negligence. In other words, I know that if I drive my car negligently, it could cause harm to other cars or people as the result of a crash. But, if some harm happens that is not a natural or probable result of my negligence, then this harm is not proximately caused by my negligence. In the previous example, I could not have reasonably foreseen that the driver of the other car would commit such a rash act as running out into traffic.

Sometimes, the duties we have are imposed by statutes or regulations, and not by common law doctrines. We will discuss the implication of these sources of law for the workplace later in this book.

Chapter 2

A Brief History of Labor and Employment Law in the United States

The Common Law Criminal Conspiracy Doctrine

The history of labor law in this country is almost as old as the nation itself. In the early years of the United States, there were few statutory laws compared to today. Most of the law was essentially made by judges who relied on legal precedents, that is, what judges decided in other cases. This principle is known as **stare decisis**. Roughly translated, it means that if the law has been declared, we will follow it.

Early American judges had little precedent of their own to follow, so they followed English law, by and large. The law in England was decidedly unfavorable to labor unions and working people in the eighteenth and nineteenth centuries. Judges in England, for the most part, were not raised in working class environments. Many people in the upper classes looked upon unions as wicked and felt threatened by them. It did not take long for the English judiciary to develop a legal doctrine to deal with the situation. It was known as the **criminal conspiracy doctrine**.

Under this doctrine, any combination of working people to raise their wages or to withhold their services (strike) was deemed to be unlawful. Further, it was a criminal wrong punishable by imprisonment. American courts were not long in adopting this legal principle and in using it against working people.

One of the earliest labor cases on the books in America concerned a group of boot makers in Philadelphia in 1805 and is known as the **Cordwainers Case** (an old term for boot maker). This group of boot makers decided to band together and present their employers with a list of compensation they demanded for making various articles of footwear. These demands included substantial pay increases. This came at a bad time for the employers because they were experiencing an onslaught of competition from the boot making shops in the newly opened frontier states and territories, which used cheaper labor. They were actually thinking about lowering prices and now, if they acceded to the boot makers' demands, they would have to raise them.

Rather than negotiate with their employees or take a strike (as would be done today), the employers chose to file criminal charges. A jury of mostly shopkeepers and businessmen was empanelled and, at the close of all of the evidence, the judge virtually instructed the jury to find the boot makers guilty of criminal conspiracy to raise wages. Not surprisingly, the jury returned a guilty verdict and the culprits were fined eight dollars each.

The criminal conspiracy doctrine did not ban one person from asking for a raise. It did outlaw, however, a group of employees banding together to ask for one. It essentially outlawed most of the central functions of labor unions: negotiating for higher pay and striking to enforce demands.

The criminal conspiracy doctrine remained in place, largely in tact, for another forty years or so when it was dealt a setback in a case in Massachusetts known as *Commonwealth v. Hunt*. In this case, the court determined that the **purpose** of the "banding together" must be looked at and if the purpose was lawful, then it was not an unlawful conspiracy for workers to group together to try to achieve it.

The criminal conspiracy doctrine was slowly eroded over time until, in 1935, the National Labor Relations Act (NLRA) abolished it altogether in one of the most significant legal turnarounds of all time. Instead of outlawing concerted action of workers to improve their wages and working conditions, the law (through the NLRA) specifically established their right to do so and afforded a means to protect that right.

Strikes and Violence

Although the nineteenth century saw a decline in the criminal conspiracy doctrine, it also saw a rise in labor strife and violence. This was particularly true after the Civil War. Although this time period saw the formation of some of the first truly national labor unions, most employers did not accept them. The short-lived National Labor Union (NLU) soon gave way to the Knights of Labor, which avoided strikes in preference for arbitration. Although the Knights successfully fought several important labor battles with railroads, by the 1890s it too had succumbed. Both the NLU and the Knights were more concerned with social and political issues than they were with wage increases for the workers they represented.

Employers reacted forcefully, and sometimes violently, to labor unions in those days. There were bitter strikes, often lasting for weeks and accompanied by violence on both sides. Sometimes, these labor disputes resembled a military operation more than what we would think of today as a strike. In one case, cannons were used by strikers to fire on strikebreakers being transported by barge down a river to a factory.

Employers not only fired union supporters, they often subjected them and their families to threats and violence. On the other side, striking workers were not above sabotage and violence themselves. Both sides occasionally committed murder.

Even though the criminal conspiracy doctrine became ineffective, workers still had no right to join a union or to engage in concerted activity to better their working conditions. In other words, they couldn't be sent to jail for being in a union, but they could be fired without any recourse to the courts. Indeed, many employers required employees to sign agreements saying that they would not join a union. If they did not sign, they would be fired. Known as **yellow dog contracts**, these agreements proved to be effective in preventing unionism in many sectors of the economy.

The end of the nineteenth century saw the birth of the American Federation of Labor. Founded in 1886, the AFL was a conglomeration of twenty-five trade unions headed by former cigar maker, Samuel Gompers. Unlike earlier national unions, the AFL did not have a long social agenda. Its main interest was wages and working conditions for its members. When asked what he wanted for his organization's members, Gompers would always reply, "More."

With the advent of the modern factory, and particularly the assembly line, more and more people were migrating to the cities to work in the large production facilities located there. The vast majority of these people were unskilled or semiskilled laborers destined to work on assembly lines, most notably in the automobile industry. These workers were shunned by the trade unions and the AFL. They found a friend, however, in labor leader John L. Lewis, a former coal miner (as well as a farmer, businessman, and construction worker) who founded the Congress of Industrial Organizations (CIO) in 1935. The CIO was to industrial unions what the AFL was to trade unions. Colorful leaders, such as Walter Reuther and Phillip Murray, emerged to take on industrial giants, such as Henry Ford and Andrew Carnegie.

The Labor Injunction

Deprived of the criminal law as a weapon to use against labor, employers in the nineteenth and twentieth centuries resorted to the courts for a different kind of assistance: the injunction. An injunction is an order from a court requiring someone to do something or to refrain from doing something. If the person under the injunction does not obey it, he/she can be made to pay a fine and/or be incarcerated. It can be a very effective tool if one knows how to use it.

Employers found the courts more than willing to enjoin labor strikes during this time period. Judges, like most people, were appalled at the violence and destruction accompanying a strike. Thus, judges believed that by enjoining the strike, they would best serve the needs of society. In actuality, they wound up serving the needs of the industrialists because, by enjoining the strike, they deprived labor of its most potent weapon.

Congress, in an attempt to help balance the scales, passed the Clayton Anti-Trust Act in 1914. Unfortunately for labor, the law contained technical flaws that rendered it virtually useless. This situation was rectified in 1932, however, with the passage of the Norris–LaGuardia Act which effectively banned federal courts from issuing injunctions in labor disputes except in certain narrow situations.

The National Labor Relations Act

The Depression in the 1930s saw the passage of several important labor laws at the federal level. One of these was the Wagner Act of 1935. President Franklin D. Roosevelt and Congress realized that organized labor could no longer be denied its place at the table in the economy. If they did not pass legislation to give the labor movement legitimacy, and at the same time lay down ground rules for labor "warfare," the economy would suffer and interstate commerce would be damaged. After an aborted attempt to pass an earlier law known as the National Recovery Act failed (due to its being declared unconstitutional by the U.S. Supreme Court), the Wagner Act (NLRA) was passed in 1935. President Roosevelt, in order to protect the Wagner Act from judicial nullification, threatened to "pack" the Supreme Court by enlarging its membership and putting friendly judges into the newly created positions. The law was upheld by the high court a few years later.

The Wagner Act gave employees the right to engage in concerted activity and prohibited employer interference with said rights. Such interference was known as an unfair labor practice. The law also created procedures for employees to select (and de-select) unions in their workplaces. Finally, the law set up the National Labor Relations Board, an administrative agency, which was empowered to enforce the law.

The Wagner Act governed labor management relations through the World War II time period. However, abuses by organized labor during the war, and the perception of many that the Wagner Act was too lopsided, led to a call for reform. This resulted in the passage of the Taft–Hartley Act in 1947. Taft–Hartley, passed over President Truman's veto, added union unfair labor practices to the employer unfair labor practices decreed by the Wagner Act. It also gave employees the explicit right to refrain from engaging in concerted activities. Finally, the law gave states the right to pass so-called "Right to Work" laws that banned union security clauses in collective bargaining agreements.

Finally, in 1957, the Landrum–Griffin Act was passed. It contained numerous provisions governing how unions could treat their members. Among these provisions was the union members' "bill of rights" that served as limitations on the union's authority to discipline members, assess dues, and control who ran for office in the union. Landrum–Griffin also required unions to prepare and file with the federal government certain reports, especially ones pertaining to union finances and use of union dues.

Together, the Wagner, Taft–Hartley, and Landrum–Griffin Acts are referred to as the National Labor Relations Act. It is the primary law governing labor–management relations in this country. The law has remained largely unchanged since the passage of Landrum–Griffin. In this book, we shall refer to the National Labor Relations Act as the NLRA. Most of the rest of this book will be about the NLRA.

The Fair Labor Standards Act of 1938

The Depression also saw the passage of another important piece of legislation. The Fair Labor Standards Act (FLSA) was passed as a direct result of the harsh economic conditions then prevailing and the destitute condition of many workers. Wages were used as a method of competition. The more you could cut wages the lower you could sell your product or the more profit you could make. Additionally, employers worked their employees in long shifts, sometimes as much as sixteen hours. Child labor was also rampant, especially in the South and in the textile mills.

The FLSA accomplished three basic things: (1) it established a minimum wage (the first minimum wage was twenty-five cents per hour), (2) it required that any employee who worked in excess of forty hours in a week be paid at time and one half his or her regular rate for all such hours in excess of forty, and (3) it banned most forms of child labor and regulated the rest. Like the NLRA, the law applied to almost all businesses and industries. The law is enforced by the Department of Labor.

Civil Rights Statutes

The NLRA and the FLSA established important rights for employees, but they did not eliminate one of the worst employment practices ever—discrimination on the basis of race, sex, religion, and national origin. We are all familiar with the history of the civil rights movement in the 1950s and 1960s in this country. One of the more important results of this turmoil was the Civil Rights Act of 1964. This law was designed to eliminate discrimination on a broad front.

Title VII prohibits discrimination in all aspects of employment based on race, sex, religion, or national origin. The law is enforced by the Equal Employment Opportunity Commission or the EEOC. This administrative agency was created by Title VII.

One year prior to the passage of the Civil Rights Act, Congress passed the Equal Pay Act. This is a narrowly drafted statute prohibiting the payment of different wages to men and women doing substantially equivalent duties. The law contains numerous exceptions for pay differences based on seniority, piece work, merit, or any other legitimate factor. Originally enforced by the Department of Labor, this law is now administered by the EEOC.

The Age Discrimination in Employment Act (ADEA) was passed in 1967. This law bans discrimination in employment based on age. Anyone forty or over is in the category protected by the law. Originally enforced by the Department of Labor, this law is also now enforced by the EEOC.

The Americans with Disabilities Act was passed in 1990. According to many, it addressed discrimination against the last sizeable minority in the United States: persons with disabilities. Both mental and physical disabilities are covered under the law. This law is also enforced by the EEOC. Amendments to the law effective in 2009 broaden the coverage of this law considerably.

Other Statutes

The Occupational Safety and Health Act (OSHA) was passed in 1970. It applies to a wide variety of industries and regulates safety in the workplace. The law is enforced by the Occupational Safety and Health Administration, a division of the Department of Labor.

The Immigration Reform and Control Act was passed in 1986. Its aim is to ensure that employers take measures to avoid hiring illegal aliens. At the same time, it forbids discrimination based on alienage (so long as the person is authorized to work in the United States).

The Employee Polygraph Protection Act of 1988 regulates the use of polygraphs in the employment context. The upshot of this law is that employers are severely restricted in the use of these devices. The law is enforced by the Department of Labor.

The Drug Free Work Place Act of 1988 applies only to federal contractors, certain depositories of federal funds, and the federal government itself. It requires covered employers to maintain policies on drug usage and to report certain convictions of employees involving drug-related offenses. This law is enforced by the various agencies awarding government monies.

The Family Medical Leave Act (FMLA) of 1993 provides certain eligible employees of covered employers with twelve weeks of unpaid leave during a twelve-month period. The leave is limited to certain medical conditions of the employee or specified family members. A recent amendment also allowed employees leave to care for certain relatives who were injured while on active duty in the U.S. armed forces. The new amendments also provide for leave to assist with financial, legal, and other issues caused by the deployment of a service member. The law is enforced by the Department of Labor.

The Uniformed Services Employment and Reemployment Rights Act (USERRA) of 1994 gives members of the armed services certain rights regarding reinstatement following service, benefit continuation, and nondiscrimination. It is enforced by the Department of Labor and Department of Justice.

Executive Order 11246 requires nondiscrimination and affirmative action for covered employers having federal contracts, depositories of federal funds, and the federal government. It is enforced by the Office of Federal Contract Compliance Programs (OFCCP), an arm of the Department of Labor.

The Bankruptcy Protection Act, 11 U.S.C. § 525, is a part of the U.S. Bankruptcy Code. It forbids discrimination against an employee solely on the basis of exercising rights under the bankruptcy law. It is enforced by the court system.

Chapter 3

Labor Law: Dealing with Labor Unions and the National Labor Relations Act

An Overview of the National Labor Relations Act (NLRA)

The three basic statutes comprising the NLRA have been discussed in Chapter 2 (the Wagner Act, Taft–Hartley Act, and Landrum–Griffin Act). It helps in understanding this statute to think of its most important three sections: 7, 8, and 9. Section 7 is the core of the law containing the basic rights of employees. Section 8 deals with unfair labor practices, both union and employer. Section 9 contains the rules on how employees elect unions or decertify unions. Although there are other sections to this law, these three are the most important by far.

As noted in the previous chapter, this law is enforced by the National Labor Relations Board (NLRB), which is composed of five members appointed by the president and approved by the Senate. They are appointed to staggered five-year terms. The Board usually decides cases in three-member panels where the majority rules. The Board is somewhat of a political animal. When Democratic members predominate, decisions predictably favor the unions. The opposite is true when Republican members are in the majority. As such, the NLRB often overrules itself, and reliance on a Board decision from years ago can sometimes be dangerous.

The NLRA also calls for the appointment of a general counsel, the chief prosecutor for the NLRB. This person is also appointed by the president and approved by the Senate. The term is four years.

Like a lot of other administrative agencies, the NLRB has divided the country into regions. Currently, there are thirty-two such regions, each of which is headed by a regional director. There is also a representative of the general counsel at each region. Within the region, there are often one or more field offices. NLRB agents are not necessarily lawyers, but often they are. Naturally, the general counsel and his/her staff are mostly composed of attorneys.

The regional director holds quite a bit of power under the regulatory scheme. He or she makes the initial determination of whether an unfair labor practice charge will go forward. The regional director also has significant power in determining whether employees will be allowed to vote on whether a union can represent them or whether an existing union will be "kicked out."

The general counsel representative will be the one prosecuting unfair labor practice charges (even though the regional director makes the determination on whether a complaint will be issued, subject to appeal if he or she refuses to issue a complaint).

Although the NLRB is empowered to issue regulations, they have not done much, at least when compared to other administrative agencies enforcing employment laws. The EEOC and OSHA, for instance, have issued multitudes of regulations dealing with the smallest details of the laws they enforce. The NLRB, with a few notable exceptions, has not issued regulations dealing with the substantive law it enforces. It has, however, issued detailed regulations and guidance on procedural issues (e.g., how unfair labor practice cases will be tried or how a labor election will be conducted).

Basic Rights of Employees

Section 7 of the NLRA is short, but important. It sets forth the rights that employees have under the law. The section reads as follows:

> Employees shall have the right to self-organization, to form, join, or assist labor organizations, to bargain collectively through representatives of their own choosing, and to engage in other concerted activities for the purpose of collective bargaining or other mutual aid or protection, and shall also have the right to refrain from any or all such activities except to the extent that such right may be affected by an agreement requiring membership in a labor organization as a condition of employment as authorized in Section 8(a)(3) [Section 158(a)(3) of this title].

There are several crucial things to remember about this section:

1. It is only employees who are being given rights, not unions or employers.
2. Employees have the right to engage in concerted activity for their mutual benefit. This means they have the right to strike. They have the right to come together as a group and petition the employer to correct grievances.
3. These rights are not given to individuals but to groups of individuals. Thus, a single employee would not be protected unless it could be shown he or she was acting on behalf of the group.
4. Employees have the right to refrain from engaging in concerted activity—they cannot be forced to strike, etc.

Section 7 rights do not depend on whether a union is present. Although the vast majority of cases involving Section 7 is in the union context, protected concerted activity can take place without a union present. This was established by the U.S. Supreme Court in a famous case arising out of the Fourth Circuit Court of Appeals in 1962, and involving the Washington Aluminum Company.* It was winter time and the employees were cold. They complained to each other bitterly about the lack of heat until finally they decided to go to the boss. When they did, they were turned away and they decided to walk out. They were fired soon thereafter. The employees persuaded the Board to pursue an unfair labor practice charge, claiming their Section 7 rights were violated. The employer defended by saying that there was no union at the plant and, therefore, the employees could not have any Section 7 rights. It was held that the employees were right. If employees engage in concerted activity, they may be protected under Section 7, even if they are not part of a union.

This is not to say that employees can do whatever they want. The employer may still discipline those who disrupt production or who commit other infractions. The employer (as we shall see later) may **replace** those who walk out. But, as we shall also see, this is different than **firing** them. This is one of those areas where the words you use can make a difference. Replacing someone and firing them may sound very similar. But, as you will see, they are quite different in the labor law context.

As noted above, it is not always clear if an employee is engaging in concerted activity, which is protected under the law. Clearly, if employees are acting as a group, it probably will be concerted activity. The issue arises, however, as to whether an individual who claims to be speaking on behalf of the group, is engaging in concerted activity. The key to this determination seems to be whether the employee doing the talking has the consent of the group for whom he is speaking. If so, the activity is concerted.

In a union setting, even individual activity to enforce or to claim rights under the collective bargaining agreement is always deemed concerted and protected. This

---

* NLRB v. Washington Aluminum Company, 370 U.S. 9 (1962).

is true even if the individual is seeking only to promote his or her own goals. If they are making a claim based on the labor agreement, the thought is that it ultimately benefits everyone because all employees benefit whenever the agreement is enforced.

Do not make the mistake in thinking that, because concerted activity is protected, you are powerless anytime a group of employees comes to you with a complaint or a "spokesperson" comes to you. You can tell these people to get back to work and, if they do not, you can take disciplinary action. What you cannot do is fire them because they came to you with a complaint.

This seems simple enough. Some things, however, have been held to constitute concerted activity that we would not normally think would fall into that category. For instance, many employers have rules prohibiting two employees from talking about how much they are paid. The National Labor Relations Board has ruled that two employees sharing wage information can constitute concerted activity because the "information exchange" may be just a preliminary to approaching the employer with a complaint about wage disparity or something of that nature. Rules against "harassment," if not properly drafted, have been declared invalid because they discourage employees from trying to persuade other employees to join (or not to join) a union.

Please note in reading Section 7 of the law, that employees not only have the right to engage in concerted activity, they have a right to **refrain** from engaging in such activity. This means that no one can force an employee to strike, go to a union meeting, or solicit for the union. We will discuss later when employees may be forced to pay union dues and the impact of so-called "Right to Work" laws.

Unfair Labor Practices

Unfair Labor Practices (sometimes referred to as "ULPs") are actions that interfere with or diminish employee rights under Section 7 of the National Labor Relations Act. They may be committed by either employers or unions. They are found in Section 8 of the Act. It is important to know that unfair labor practices may only be committed by employers or unions. One employee cannot commit a ULP against another employee. Of course, supervisors, in the eyes of the law, are "the employer." As you might expect, most unfair labor practice allegations concern conduct allegedly committed by supervisors or managers.

Employer Unfair Labor Practices

Below is an excerpt from Section 8(a) of the law that details employer unfair labor practices.

> It shall be an unfair labor practice for an employer—
> (1) to interfere with, restrain, or coerce employees in the exercise of the rights guaranteed in Section 7 [Section 157 of this title];

(2) to dominate or interfere with the formation or administration of any labor organization or contribute financial or other support to it: *Provided*, That subject to rules and regulations made and published by the Board pursuant to Section 6 [Section 156 of this title], an employer shall not be prohibited from permitting employees to confer with him during working hours without loss of time or pay;

(3) by discrimination in regard to hire or tenure of employment or any term or condition of employment to encourage or discourage membership in any labor organization: *Provided*, That nothing in this Act [subchapter], or in any other statute of the United States, shall preclude an employer from making an agreement with a labor organization (not established, maintained, or assisted by any action defined in Section 8(a) of this Act [in this subsection] as an unfair labor practice) to require as a condition of employment membership therein on or after the thirtieth day following the beginning of such employment or the effective date of such agreement, whichever is the later, (i) if such labor organization is the representative of the employees as provided in Section 9(a) [Section 159(a) of this title], in the appropriate collective-bargaining unit covered by such agreement when made, and (ii) unless following an election held as provided in Section 9(e) [Section 159(e) of this title] within one year preceding the effective date of such agreement, the Board shall have certified that at least a majority of the employees eligible to vote in such election have voted to rescind the authority of such labor organization to make such an agreement: *Provided further*, That no employer shall justify any discrimination against an employee for non-membership in a labor organization (A) if he has reasonable grounds for believing that such membership was not available to the employee on the same terms and conditions generally applicable to other members, or (B) if he has reasonable grounds for believing that membership was denied or terminated for reasons other than the failure of the employee to tender the periodic dues and the initiation fees uniformly required as a condition of acquiring or retaining membership;

(4) to discharge or otherwise discriminate against an employee because he has filed charges or given testimony under this Act [subchapter];

(5) to refuse to bargain collectively with the representatives of his employees, subject to the provisions of Section 9(a) [Section 159(a) of this title].

Section 8(a)1 Employer Coercion of Employees

Threats

This is the section that bans employers from interfering with employees in the exercise of their Section 7 rights. One of the most common ways to violate this statute is to threaten employees with bad consequences if they support the union or if they do not oppose the union. Clearly, if you tell an employee he/she will be fired if he/she joins a union, you have committed a violation of 8(a)1.

Disguising your threats will not do you any good. For instance, if you tell an employee that his or her future will be bleak if he/she votes for the union in an election, this is also a violation. Telling an employee he/she had better not go to a union meeting "if you know what is good for you" would be a violation.

Promises of Benefits

It is also a violation of the law to promise a benefit to employees in exchange for their abandonment of the union or to otherwise give up their Section 7 rights. Sometimes these are called "bribes." For instance, promising an employee a promotion if he/she will go out and speak against the union to his or her fellow employees would be a violation. Telling an employee "things will be better for you" if he/she votes against the union is a violation.

Surveillance

Another form of 8(a)1 violation is surveillance. In other words, we cannot spy on employees to determine if they are engaged in union activities. This does not mean you cannot observe employees when they are at work. What it does mean is you cannot sit outside a union hall and take notes of who attends. You cannot hide in a closet in the break room in hopes of hearing about union activity. You cannot install listening devices or hidden cameras if your aim is to gain information about the union sentiments of your employees.

Impression of Surveillance

An interesting (and sometimes puzzling) offshoot of surveillance is that we cannot give employees the impression we have put them under surveillance, even if we have not in fact done so. For instance, telling an employee that "we have been watching you and we know who the union leaders are" would be unlawful even if the statement were not true because we are giving employees the impression we are spying on them.

Interrogation

We cannot go up to an employee and ask him or her if they support the union, who are the union leaders, how many will vote for the union, where or when the next union meeting will be, etc. Such questioning is considered to tend to restrain employees in the exercise of their Section 7 rights.

Asking and listening, however, are two different things. If you go up to an employee and ask him how he is doing and he starts to relate information about the union, you can certainly listen and pass this along to your boss. You cannot, however, start asking questions even if the employee is the one who brings up the subject.

There are a few exceptions to this rule, such as where the supervisor and the employee are closely related or where the conversation takes place in the employee's home, instead of in the supervisor's office. It is best, however, not to try to rely on any exception and play strictly by the rules. **If you have a good rapport with your employees, you will find out all you need to know about what is going on in your area. You do not have to violate the law to get information**.

Section 8(c)—The "Free Speech" Proviso

When the Wagner Act was first passed, it was interpreted by many to mean employers could not voice their opinions about unions or talk about the disadvantages of unionization. When the Taft–Hartley Act was passed in 1947, a section was added to the National Labor Relations Act that made it clear that employers could "speak up" about unions. This is Section 8(c) of the Act, often known as the "free speech proviso." It reads as follows:

> The expressing of any views, argument, or opinion, or the dissemination thereof, whether in written, printed, graphic, or visual form, shall not constitute or be evidence of an unfair labor practice under any of the provisions of this Act [subchapter], if such expression contains no threat of reprisal or force or promise of benefit.

Distilled down to its basics, this section allows employers to express opinions, views, or arguments and to disseminate those in any form so long as they do not contain a threat or bribe.

It is often difficult to distinguish between an opinion and a threat. The easy way to remember the difference is to think of the difference between the words "could" and "will."

If I tell my employees that if a union comes into the plant, there could be a strike, I am merely telling them about a possibility. If I tell them a strike *will* happen, then I am making a threat (or at least that is how the law interprets it).

What all this means it that you can give your opinion about the union in the most explicit and direct way, so long as you don't threaten or bribe. There are some exceptions, of course. For instance, you should not appeal to racial prejudice or incite violence. You should be honest, although the law does not necessarily require this.

What are some more examples of what you *can* say? You could tell employees that unions at other companies have caused harm to those companies. You could tell them about corruption in unions and provide them with newspaper clippings demonstrating this. You could tell them about union seniority rules and the implication this *could* have for the principle that one should be promoted on merit, and not on the basis of how long they have been around the plant. You could tell them that you don't believe the union is in the best interest of the company. You could tell them about your own experiences with unions in the past. You can tell them about the realities of collective bargaining and that having a union does not always mean they will get "more" (we will discuss the collective bargaining process in some detail later in this book). You can tell them about union finances and how much unions take into their coffers, where it comes from, and how it is spent.

In deciding what you can or should say to employees, you need to be aware of a legal principle called the "futility doctrine." If you tell employees that the company will never reach a contract with the union or that the union will never do the employees any good or that the company will never recognize the union, you may have committed a violation of 8(a)1. The NLRB has ruled that such statements give the employees the impression that electing the union or engaging in their Section 7 rights would do them no good and violates the law. It is alright to say that the union has disadvantages and *could* cause troubles. It is not alright to say that there is *no way* that employees could benefit from the union. The rationale for the rule seems to be that the latter statement is more akin to a threat, which, as you now know, is prohibited by Section 8(a)(1) and not protected by Section 8(c).

Section 8(a)(2) Employer Interference or Domination of a Labor Union

Section 8(a)(2) prohibits employer domination or interference with a labor organization. It also prohibits employer contributions of financial support or other forms of support to a labor organization.

This section of the law stems mainly from the early practice of forming "company unions." In the 1920s and 1930s, employers faced with the prospect of a union organizational drive would merely create their own, internal unions that would go through sham bargaining for a contract that would be quite favorable to the employer. On other occasions, a company would dominate a weak union with bribes and other financial incentives to the union's officers. Because this practice deprived employees of the right to freely choose the union they wanted under Section 7, it was declared to be one of the unfair labor practices created by the law.

There are very few "company unions" today in the classic sense of the word. Sometimes, employee committees formed by the company in a nonunion setting are deemed unlawful under Section 8(a)(2). This is in part because such committees can fall within the definition of a "labor organization" and, if the employer forms them and/ or tells them what they are going to talk about, etc., they could run afoul of the law.

The law defines a labor organization as follows:

> The term *labor organization* means any organization of any kind, or any agency or employee representation committee or plan, in which employees participate and which exists for the purpose, in whole or in part, of dealing with employers concerning grievances, labor disputes, wages, rates of pay, hours of employment, or conditions of work.

Particular problems are created if the committee actually negotiates with the employer over terms and conditions of employment. The clearest case would be an employee committee created to suggest to the employer whether it should give a wage increase. Other examples of unlawful committees would be where a committee was created to come up with an absentee policy. On the other hand, if the committee does not "deal with" the employer in the sense of negotiation, but comes up with various options without recommending any, it may be lawful. "Think tanks" and quality circles usually do not violate the law. Self-contained work teams that decide how they are going to get work done are usually lawful as well.

If a committee has been delegated a management function, then such a committee is lawful. Let us say the employer created a peer review committee that either approves or can overturn discipline. In this case, the committee *decides*; it does not negotiate.

Please note that the only time such committees may violate the law is usually when there is no union at the workplace. When a union is in the picture, such committees are formed either with the cooperation or the acquiescence of the union and, as such, are not considered company dominated labor organizations.

If you work in a nonunion establishment, it is best to seek competent legal advice before forming any committee in which employees participate and which will be charged with making suggestions about working conditions, pay, or the like.

Section 8(a)(3) Discrimination

Section 8(a)(3) prohibits discrimination against an employee in order to encourage or discourage membership in a labor organization. The text reads in relevant part as follows:

> ... by discrimination in regard to hire or tenure of employment or any term or condition of employment to encourage or discourage membership in any labor organization: *Provided*, That nothing in this Act [subchapter], or in any other statute of the United States, shall preclude an employer from making an agreement with a labor organization (not established, maintained, or assisted by any action defined in Section 8(a) of this Act [in this subsection] as an unfair labor practice) to require as a condition of employment membership therein on or after the thirtieth

day following the beginning of such employment or the effective date of such agreement, whichever is the later, (i) if such labor organization is the representative of the employees as provided in Section 9(a) [Section 159(a) of this title], in the appropriate collective-bargaining unit covered by such agreement when made, and (ii) unless following an election held as provided in Section 9(e) [Section 159(e) of this title] within one year preceding the effective date of such agreement, the Board shall have certified that at least a majority of the employees eligible to vote in such election have voted to rescind the authority of such labor organization to make such an agreement: *Provided further,* That no employer shall justify any discrimination against an employee for non-membership in a labor organization (A) if he has reasonable grounds for believing that such membership was not available to the employee on the same terms and conditions generally applicable to other members, or (B) if he has reasonable grounds for believing that membership was denied or terminated for reasons other than the failure of the employee to tender the periodic dues and the initiation fees uniformly required as a condition of acquiring or retaining membership ...

The first thing to note about this section is that something must be done to an employee. Second, the thing done must be adverse or detrimental to the employee. Third, the motive of the employer must be in substantial part, to encourage or discourage membership in a union or union activity.

A clear example would be if a company fired an employee because he or she was the main union organizer in the plant. Another example would be where a known union supporter was disciplined more harshly for performance problems compared to employees who were not union supporters, but who committed substantially similar offenses. For example, if you issue a union organizer a written reprimand for missing work three times in a month, but an employee who is known to be against the union gets only a verbal warning for missing work three times in a month. Unless the employer can prove a legitimate business related reason for the difference, an inference may be drawn that the union supporter was treated more harshly because of his/her union affiliation.

Because the employer's motive is usually in question here, these cases are proved by direct evidence of the motive or indirect evidence. Direct evidence usually consists of statements made by management officials (often first-line supervisors) who reveal the employer's motive in a direct sense. For instance, if a supervisor were overheard to say, "We got rid of Joe because he was a union supporter," this would constitute direct evidence of the employer's motive. In the eyes of the law, a supervisor's statement is the same as the statement of the company.

Not all statements, however, need to be quite this direct in order to constitute "direct evidence" of illegal motive. Thus, if the supervisor had said, "That union supporter Joe got what he deserved," or even, "Joe got what he deserved," could be construed as direct evidence that the employer "got back" at Joe for being a union supporter.

Not surprisingly, most cases of discrimination are proven by *indirect* evidence. This could be loosely characterized as "circumstantial evidence."

For instance, if the company deviates from its own policies in firing a union supporter, the administrative law judge could infer that it did so in order to "get" the person. There may be other legal reasons for deviating from policy, but the inference could still be made. Similarly—and as alluded to above—if the company treated the union supporter more harshly than nonsupporters for the same "offense" or behavior, the inference could be made that this was the result of antiunion motives. The principle of "treat like cases alike" or equality of treatment is your best protection here. If you are going to deviate from policy, make an exception, or go beyond what is customary, make sure you have a good reason for doing so and that your reasoning and the facts on which it is based are well documented.

Naturally, before you can be accused of discrimination, it must be proved that you knew the alleged victim was a union supporter or had advocated on the part of the union. Often, this is not an issue since the sentiments of many union advocates are displayed openly. Often, statements of supervisors are used to attribute knowledge of union support to the employer. This is why it is wise not to speculate openly about who is or is not a union supporter. Express your opinions about "who is and who isn't" a union supporter in management meetings, but not on the shop floor.

The courts and the NLRB have held that if a company can show it would have taken the same action against an employee regardless of whether he or she was a union supporter, it is a defense to an 8(a)(3) charge. For instance, if Joe, an ardent union supporter, is walking around the plant talking to others when he should be working, you can discipline him so long as you would discipline a nonunion supporter for doing the same thing. The discipline given to Joe, moreover, must be proportional to that given to others in the past for the same or similar offenses. So, if you fire Joe, but have only warned others in the past for leaving their workstations, it might look like you have singled out Joe for harsher treatment because of his union support. Naturally, it is legitimate to take into consideration the employee's record, whether it is his/her first offense, and other special circumstances. Truly, no two cases are alike. Nevertheless, the NLRB and the courts will become very suspicious if union supporters are disciplined for committing certain acts when nonunion supporters are not so-disciplined.

Discrimination also can arise in areas other than discipline. For instance, if Joe (the union supporter) is in line for a promotion, but it is given to someone else who is arguably less qualified, this could raise the specter of discrimination. Please do not be confused. Under the law, you can promote whomever you want, but you cannot do so on an illegal basis, such as union support.

Discrimination can arise in the hiring arena as well. If you refuse to hire someone because he or she has been a union member at a previous job, you may well be guilty of discrimination in violation of 8(a)(3).

To make things even harder for employers, it is not necessary for a charging party to prove that his/her union support was the *only* reason for the discrimination. It is enough to prove that the union activity played an important part in the employer's decision to take the action that it did.

It is also unlawful (although very rare) for an employer to discriminate against someone because they are *not* a union supporter. Remember, Section 7 of the Act gives employees the equal right to support or not support a labor organization. The only exception to this rule arises in the case of what is known as a "union security clause" in a labor contract between company and union. Such clauses require all employees to become members of the union and remain a member in good standing as a condition of employment. This concept of "membership," however, has been defined narrowly. Basically, for purposes of Section 8(a)(3), it means the requirement that the employee pay regular dues and assessments. It does not mean that the employee has to actually become a member in the sense that he or she takes the oath of loyalty to the union or has to attend meetings. If, however, an employee under a union security clause does not pay regular dues or assessments, the union can demand that the employer fire that individual. Such terminations, although discriminatory against a nonunion supporter, are specifically excepted from the operation of 8(a)(3), and are lawful. Please note that union security clauses are not lawful in all states. The Taft–Hartley Act allowed states to pass what are known as Right to Work laws. Such laws make union security clauses unlawful. For a list of states that had Right to Work laws as of this writing, see Appendix 1.

Remember, consistency in discipline cannot only keep you out of trouble, it also is just good business.

Section 8(a)(4) Retaliation for Participating in Board Proceedings or for Filing Charge

This section is fairly straightforward:

> … to discharge or otherwise discriminate against an employee because
> he has filed charges or given testimony under this Act …

The purpose of Section 8(a)(4) is to protect the integrity of NLRB proceedings. If someone could be retaliated against for filing an unfair labor practice charge or for cooperating with the Board in an investigation or testifying at a hearing, then the legitimacy of the process would be in jeopardy.

This section prohibits two things: discharge or discrimination. Discharge means to fire or it could be "constructive discharge," which means to intentionally make someone's job so miserable or untenable that no reasonable person would be expected to stay. An example of this would be to take away someone's job duties and assign him or her extremely unpleasant chores, yelling at someone all the time, belittling him/her in front of co-workers constantly, severely reducing his/her pay or taking away benefits. Discrimination is the same thing we learned about in the preceding section pertaining to 8(a)(3).

The protected activities are basically filing an unfair labor practice charge or participating in Board proceedings. This law has been held to protect employees who are interviewed by Board agents in connection with their official duties. The investigation does not necessarily have to be regarding an unfair labor practice allegation. It could be regarding an investigation into an election petition, a petition for injunctive relief, or other Board processes.

If you are about to discipline someone who has filed a charge, given testimony in a Board proceeding, or cooperated in a Board investigation, make sure you can prove that your reasons are legitimate and have nothing to do with protected activity. As in any type of retaliation claim, the closer in time between the protected activity and the adverse action, the stronger the inference that retaliation is present. The greater the time period, the less strong the inference. For instance, if an employee was fired a week after giving testimony at a Board hearing, the presumption may be strong that the employee suffered retaliation. On the other hand, if the employee was fired a year after testifying, you would have a hard time convincing the Board that the firing was motivated by the testimony.

Many factors can come to play in retaliation cases. In addition to timing, there is the factor (discussed above) of consistency in treatment. Is the employer treating like cases alike? Statements made, often by supervisors such as you, can either help or hurt the employer's cause. For instance, stating that an employee is a "troublemaker" because he filed a charge or that she is "disloyal" because she testified against the company in a hearing, could be used as evidence that adverse action against an employee was motivated by a desire to retaliate.

Section 8(a)(5) Refusal to Bargain in Good Faith

This section requires that the employer bargain in "good faith" with the representative of its employees:

> ... to refuse to bargain collectively with the representatives of his employees, subject to the provisions of Section 9(a) [Section 159(a) of this title].

This section has been amplified by the addition of Section 8(d) in 1947:

> Obligation to Bargain Collectively

> For the purposes of this section, to bargain collectively is the performance of the mutual obligation of the employer and the representative

of the employees to meet at reasonable times and confer in good faith with respect to wages, hours, and other terms and conditions of employment, or the negotiation of an agreement, or any question arising thereunder, and the execution of a written contract incorporating any agreement reached if requested by either party, but such obligation does not compel either party to agree to a proposal or require the making of a concession: *Provided*, That where there is in effect a collective bargaining contract covering employees in an industry affecting commerce, the duty to bargain collectively shall also mean that no party to such contract shall terminate or modify such contract, unless the party desiring such termination or modification—

(1) serves a written notice upon the other party to the contract of the proposed termination or modification sixty days prior to the expiration date thereof, or in the event such contract contains no expiration date, sixty days prior to the time it is proposed to make such termination or modification;

(2) offers to meet and confer with the other party for the purpose of negotiating a new contract or a contract containing the proposed modifications;

(3) notifies the Federal Mediation and Conciliation Service within thirty days after such notice of the existence of a dispute, and simultaneously therewith notifies any State or Territorial agency established to mediate and conciliate disputes within the State or Territory where the dispute occurred, provided no agreement has been reached by that time; and

(4) continues in full force and effect, without resorting to strike or lock-out, all the terms and conditions of the existing contract for a period of sixty days after such notice is given or until the expiration date of such contract, whichever occurs later.

This is one of the trickiest sections of the law in terms of the difficulties it has caused both employers and unions. Fortunately, most first-line supervisors do not become involved in bargaining for a contract, so you don't have to worry too much about that aspect of Section 8(a)(5). Even so, we will discuss it at length later. There are other parts of this section, however, that may concern you more directly.

Basically, this part of the law requires an employer to do several things once a union is certified by the Board to be the collective bargaining representative of some or all of the company's employees. First, the employer must be willing to sit down with the union and attempt to negotiate a collective bargaining agreement. Section 8d of the law makes clear that this means a willingness to meet at reasonable times and confer in good faith with regard to wages, hours of work, and other terms and conditions of employment. It also requires that the employer be willing to reduce any agreement reached to a written form and sign it. Finally, it requires negotiation of matters or disputes that arise under a collective bargaining agreement once one is negotiated. This includes the obligation to discuss grievances with the union.

Section 8d does not require, however, that either side make any particular concession or that they even come to an agreement at all (whether on a labor contract or the resolution of a grievance arising under a labor contract). All it requires is that the company negotiate with a sincere desire to reach an agreement, if one can be reached.

A reading of Section 8d makes it clear that the obligation to bargain in good faith is a *mutual* obligation imposed on the union as well as the company. As we shall see later, union bad faith bargaining is a union unfair labor practice.

Section 8d also contains certain notice requirements imposed on a party desiring to terminate or modify a labor agreement once its expiration date has arrived. Specifically, the party desiring to terminate or modify must notify the other party of its desire at least sixty days before the termination date. It is also required that the party desiring to terminate or modify the contract must notify the Federal Mediation and Conciliation Service (FMCS) at least thirty days after serving the sixty-day notice mentioned above. All notifications must be in writing. The notice to the FMCS may be found on its Web site: http://www.fmcs.gov/internet/. The FMCS is a federal agency tasked with helping parties mediate contract disputes. It also supplies lists of arbitrators for the parties to use in resolving disputes that arise under a collective bargaining agreement.

Most parties send out both notices at least sixty days in advance. Sometimes the contract requires greater notice and, if this is the case, you should comply with the contract provisions.

The duty to bargain also includes the requirement that the employer furnish the union with certain information that is necessary for the union to have to adequately represent its bargaining unit members. This might include wage information or information about employee benefits (such as health insurance costs) for bargaining purposes. As will be explained later, it is because of this rule that employers should take care what reasons they give the union for refusing pay or benefit increases. If the employer says it "cannot afford" to increase pay and benefits, it may have to produce its books and records to the union so the union can determine for itself the truth of the employer's claim. (This is sometimes known as "pleading poverty.") On the other hand, if the employer asserts that it will not give the increases demanded by the union because they are too high compared to other employers in the industry or in the area, the union would not have the right to inspect the employer's books. The duty to supply information arises only when the union requests it. If the union does not ask, there is generally no duty to provide it.

The duty to supply information also arises in the context of grievances filed under the grievance and arbitration provisions of the collective bargaining agreement. Even though the language of the contract may not mention the duty to provide information, Section 8(a)(5) and the court and Board decisions interpreting it require the employer to provide the union with information it needs to process the grievance in question. Once again, the duty to provide information in such circumstances arises only when the union requests it.

For instance, if an employee has been terminated for theft, it is quite common for the union to request statements taken from witnesses, supervisor notes of the investigation, and the employee's personnel file. If the union believes the employee in question might have been treated more harshly than others who have committed the same infraction, they may ask for the disciplinary records of other employees. We will discuss the limits of such rights elsewhere in this book. Suffice it to say here that the Board and the courts have given the unions every benefit of the doubt when it comes to such information requests. Failure to provide the information requested could lead to an 8(a)(5) charge.

Union Unfair Labor Practices

We will not spend as much time discussing union unfair labor practices compared to the time spent discussing the ones that can be committed by employers. First, there are not really as many ways a union can get into trouble compared to the employer. Second, the overwhelming number of charges that are filed are under Section 8(a), employer unfair labor practices. Union unfair labor practices are found in Section 8(b) of the NLRA.

One thing that is important to note about union unfair labor practices is that they can only be committed by a union *or its agent*. Although this is true of employer unfair labor practices as well, the concept bears a little more explaining in the context of union unfair labor practices. Usually, the actions of a rank and file employee who is a union member cannot be attributed to the union without some proof that the acts were authorized by the union. The bottom line is that to successfully charge a union with an unfair labor practice, you have to prove that the act was committed by an agent of the union (such as the business agent, union president) or that the act was authorized by such a person. Sometimes this is difficult to prove. For instance, if two rank and file employees who are union supporters beat up one of your employees because he has spoken out against the union, it may be hard to get enough evidence to prove that the act was authorized by a union agent. Of course, you can discipline the two employees involved, but the union itself may escape the consequences.

Section 8(b)(1)(A) Union Coercion of Employees

It shall be an unfair labor practice for a labor organization or its agents:

> (1) to restrain or coerce (A) employees in the exercise of the rights guaranteed in Section 7 [Section 157 of this title]: *Provided*, That this paragraph shall not impair the right of a labor organization to prescribe its own rules with respect to the acquisition or retention of membership therein …

This section prohibits coercion and restraint exercised by unions against employees. As you may recall, employees have the right under Section 7 to *refrain* from engaging in concerted activities or union support. A common situation addressed by Section 8(b)(1)(A) is violence or threats of violence. For example, a union business agent who threatens to physically harm an employee if he crosses a picket line violates the law.

Of course, actual violence is also a violation. There have even been some cases where union violence against nonemployees in connection with a labor dispute have been held to violate the Section if employees are likely to know about the violence and be deterred by it from exercising their rights.

This section also can be violated by union fines levied against employees **in some instances**. If a fine is levied for testifying against the union in a Board proceeding, such would violate the law. On the other hand, fining or expelling an employee for crossing a legal picket line would not violate the law. The law allows the union to impose discipline in furtherance of legitimate union interests. For instance, the union may expel a member who files a decertification petition (but may not fine him). The employer is not compelled, however, to discharge an employee who is expelled from the union for any reason other than nonpayment of regular dues and fees. Also, if an employee resigns from the union before he or she crosses the picket line (or commits some other act that violates union rules), the enforcement of the fine by the union against the member may be impossible.

Often, the employer needs to have a bargaining unit member testify at an arbitration proceeding to prove its case. The employee, for instance, might have been a witness to the act giving rise to discipline against another bargaining unit member. Unions often view such testimony as an act of disloyalty. It is against the law, however, for the union to threaten to fine a member for such testimony.

You may hear of instances of conduct by the union against one of your employees that you believe may violate Section 8(b)(1)(A). There is usually very little you can do about it on your own, and you probably should not attempt to (unless it is an emergency situation). Such situations should be reported through your chain of command. The company must be careful in such situations not to overstep its legitimate powers.

Section 8(b)(1)(B) Union Coercion of Employer in the Selection of Its Representatives

It shall be an unfair labor practice for a labor organization or its agents:

> (1) to restrain or coerce *** (B) an employer in the selection of his representatives for the purposes of collective bargaining or the adjustment of grievances …

This section prohibits union interference with the company's choice of its representatives who deal with the union. The company has the right to choose its own representatives who deal with the union in the areas of collective bargaining and grievance adjustment. Union actions designed to force the employer to change its representatives or action directed against the representative himself or herself could violate this section.

At times, a supervisor will have been a part of the bargaining unit and a union member prior to his or her promotion. Many such supervisors retain their membership in the union in some form or fashion. On occasions the union has attempted to fine the supervisor in his or her capacity as a union member for doing things which the union does not like; for instance, if the supervisor denies a grievance or takes a hard stand at the bargaining table. Such activities violate Section 8(b)(1)(B).

Section 8(b)(2) Union Attempts to Cause an Employer to Discriminate Against an Employee

It is an unfair labor practice:

> (2) to cause or attempt to cause an employer to discriminate against an employee in violation of subsection (a)(3) [of subsection (a)(3) of this section] or to discriminate against an employee with respect to whom membership in such organization has been denied or terminated on some ground other than his failure to tender the periodic dues and the initiation fees uniformly required as a condition of acquiring or retaining membership …

As you may recall, Section 8(a)(3) prohibits employer discrimination against an employee based on that employees exercise of Section 7 rights. Section 8(b)(2) makes it unlawful for a union to "cause or attempt to cause" an employer to violate Section 8(a)(3). Thus, if a union attempts to have the employer discharge an employee for crossing a picket line, this would violate the section. This section is also involved in union efforts to squelch dissent within union ranks. For instance, a union might be tempted to try to persuade the employer to discriminate against a member who is a gadfly at union meetings or who is running for union office against an entrenched incumbent.

A major exception to the proscriptions of Section 8(b)(2) involves union security clauses. Except in a Right to Work state, unions and companies can agree to a contract provision requiring all bargaining unit employees to "become union members and remain in good standing with the union" as a condition of employment or continued employment. Such clauses are known by a variety of terms, but we will call them union security clauses. It is not a violation of Section 8(b)(2) for a union to require an employer to discharge an employee for failure to pay regular dues and fees. The payment of such items, however, is all that is required to be "in good standing." The union may be able to fine employees or expel them for other behaviors or acts considered to be in contravention of union rules, but the union cannot require the employer to fire employees in such cases.

A union violates Section 8(b)(2) if it refuses to refer a person for employment from a hiring hall because he or she is not a union member or because he or she has instituted internal complaints against the union.

Section 8(b)(3) Union Duty to Bargain in Good Faith

It is an unfair labor practice for a union:

> (3) to refuse to bargain collectively with an employer, provided it is the representative of his employees subject to the provisions of Section 9(a) [Section 159(a) of this title] ...

The union has a reciprocal duty to bargain in good faith with the employer just as the employer has an obligation to bargain with the union. This includes the duty to furnish information, as previously discussed in connection with the employer's duty to bargain. It also includes the duty to notify the employer of a desire to terminate or modify the agreement under Section 8(d).

Section 8(b)(4) Secondary Activity

It is an unfair labor practice for a union:

> (4) (i) to engage in, or to induce or encourage any individual employed by any person engaged in commerce or in an industry affecting commerce to engage in, a strike or a refusal in the course of his employment to use, manufacture, process, transport, or otherwise handle or work on any goods, articles, materials, or commodities or to perform any services; or (ii) to threaten, coerce, or restrain any person engaged in commerce or in an industry affecting commerce, where in either case an object thereof is—
>
> (A) forcing or requiring any employer or self-employed person to join any labor or employer organization or to enter into any agreement which is prohibited by subsection (e) of this section;
>
> (B) forcing or requiring any person to cease using, selling, handling, transporting, or otherwise dealing in the products of any other producer, processor, or manufacturer; or to cease doing business with any other person, or forcing or requiring any other employer to recognize or bargain with a labor organization as the representative of his employees unless such labor organization has been certified as the representative of such employees under the provisions of section 159 of this title: *Provided,* That nothing contained in this clause (B) shall be construed to make unlawful, where not otherwise unlawful, any primary strike or primary picketing;
>
> (C) forcing or requiring any employer to recognize or bargain with a particular labor organization as the representative of his employees if another labor organization has been certified as the representative of such employees under the provisions of section 159 of this title;

(D) forcing or requiring any employer to assign particular work to employees in a particular labor organization or in a particular trade, craft, or class rather than to employees in another labor organization or in another trade, craft, or class, unless such employer is failing to conform to an order or certification of the Board determining the bargaining representative for employees performing such work.

This is a rather complicated section of the Act and has been the subject of many decisions of both Board and courts. Basically, it prohibits a union from trying to gain leverage in a dispute with an employer by bringing certain types of pressure on those who deal with the employer. The employer with whom the union has the dispute is known as the "primary employer." The employer or entity the union is trying to pressure is known as the "secondary employer." Usually, this takes the form of trying to persuade the employees of the secondary employer to cease working in order to bring pressure on the secondary employer to persuade the primary employer to give in to union demands. Basically, this section prohibits unions from trying to involve neutral employers in a labor dispute. For instance, if a union sets up a picket line around the premises of an employer with whom the primary employer does business, a violation of Section 8(b)(4) has occurred. An exception to this rule is known as the "ally doctrine." This is when a struck, primary employer sends work that would normally have been done by striking employees to another employer.

This section of the law often comes into play when there is more than one employer at a work site, such as a construction project, or when an employer is "ambulatory," such as when its delivery trucks are parked at another employer's facility while unloading or picking up cargo. In such cases, employers often set up a "reserved gate" through which the primary employer's employees must enter and leave. Picketing would be lawful at that gate, only so long as the primary's employees do not use other gates. If they do, the gates become "tainted" and may be picketed notwithstanding the fact that employees of secondary employers also use the gate.

Typically, Section 8(b)(4) applies only to picketing and similar conduct. It will usually not apply to leafleting or handbilling, which is directed to the consumer and customers asking them not to buy certain products sold by the neutral employer. The handbill must truthfully advise the public of the nature of the primary dispute and the secondary employer's relationship to the dispute (e.g., it sells goods produced by the primary employer) so long as it does not substantially depart from fact or attempt to deceive.

Of course, such handbilling must be peaceful in nature, and not accompanied by picketing. If, however, the handbilling is directed toward the employees of the neutral employer, it may violate the Act.

Usually, the company can prohibit handbilling by nonemployee union organizers anywhere on its property. This right may be lost, however, where the employer allows similar activity by other groups, even charitable groups like the Salvation Army.

Section 8(b)(6) Featherbedding

It is an unfair labor practice for a union:

> (6) to cause or attempt to cause an employer to pay or deliver or agree to pay or deliver any money or other thing of value, in the nature of an exaction, for services which are not performed or not to be performed …

Although not now a common occurrence, unions have been known in the past to coerce employers to pay people for doing nothing. We are not talking about those situations when employees get "reporting pay" or "call in pay." These are lawful provisions found in many collective bargaining agreements. Similarly, the prohibition against featherbedding does not extend to bona fide lunch breaks, coffee breaks, and the like.

Featherbedding, as that term is defined under law, is when a union makes (or tries to make) an employer pay for services that have not been performed and will not be performed. For instance, if a musicians' union required an employer to pay for musicians who never show up, such would violate the law. Another example of featherbedding would be where the union required the employer to engage a union steward who didn't do any work at the job site.

On the other hand, forcing an employer to pay for services that, even though useless or undesired by the employer, are actually performed is not a violation of the statute. This is sometimes known as "make work." As distasteful and inefficient as such practices may sometimes be, they are not illegal if an employer agrees to them.

Section 8(b)(7) Recognitional Picketing

It is an unfair labor practice for a union:

> (7) to picket or cause to be picketed, or threaten to picket or cause to be picketed, any employer where an object thereof is forcing or requiring an employer to recognize or bargain with a labor organization as the representative of his employees, or forcing or requiring the employees of an employer to accept or select such labor organization as their collective-bargaining representative, unless such labor organization is currently certified as the representative of such employees …

This section is designed to limit the time a union can picket to force an employer to recognize it as the exclusive bargaining agent of its employees. There are several restrictions and exceptions to this rule.

First, it applies only to picketing and not to handbilling (the handing out of leaflets, flyers, brochures, and the like).

Second, it applies only to picketing that has as its object the organization of the employer's employees and/or forcing the employer to recognize the union. It does not apply to picketing for other reasons, including "area standards" picketing. This is picketing designed to inform the public that the employer pays what the union considers are substandard wages in the local area. It does not apply to picketing that protests unfair labor practices or unlawful discharges.

Third, the union may picket for recognition for up to thirty days without a petition for an election being filed. If they file a petition, they may continue to picket after that time. There are some exceptions to the thirty-day limit and injunctions have been sought against the union in cases where the picketing was less than thirty days.

Fourth, if a valid labor election has been held at your facility, a union may not picket for recognition for a period of twelve months from the date of the Board's certification of the results of the election.

Fifth, the union may not engage in recognitional picketing when another union is currently certified. There are some limitations on this rule, applying mainly when a question concerning representation can be raised, such as the "window period" when a petition by a rival union could be filed. This "window" is discussed below in the section entitled "Contract Bar."

Section 8(e) Hot Cargo Agreements

(e) **[Enforceability of contract or agreement to boycott any other employer; exception]** It shall be an unfair labor practice for any labor organization and any employer to enter into any contract or agreement, express or implied, whereby such employer ceases or refrains or agrees to cease or refrain from handling, using, selling, transporting or otherwise dealing in any of the products of any other employer, or cease doing business with any other person, and any contract or agreement entered into heretofore or hereafter containing such an agreement shall be to such extent unenforceable and void: *Provided,* That nothing in this subsection (e) [this subsection] shall apply to an agreement between a labor organization and an employer in the construction industry relating to the contracting or subcontracting of work to be done at the site of the construction, alteration, painting, or repair of a building, structure, or other work: *Provided further,* That for the purposes of this subsection (e) and Section 8(b)(4)(B) [this subsection and Subsection (b)(4)(B) of this section] the terms "any employer," "any person engaged in commerce or an industry affecting commerce," and "any person" when used in relation to the terms "any other producer, processor, or manufacturer," "any other employer," or "any other person" shall not include persons in the relation of a jobber, manufacturer, contractor, or subcontractor working on the goods or premises of the jobber or manufacturer or performing parts of an integrated process of production in the apparel and clothing industry: *Provided further,* That nothing in this Act [subchapter] shall prohibit the enforcement of any agreement which is within the foregoing exception.

This section is actually a prohibition on both company and union. This section prohibits agreements between union and company whereby the company agrees not to do business with another person or company or not to handle or use the products of another person or company. The application of this section is severely limited in the construction and garment industries.

The gist of the prohibition is against secondary objects, as opposed to protecting the work of bargaining unit members. For instance, a prohibition on subcontracting bargaining unit work to another company would not violate Section 8(e). On the other hand, forcing an employer to cease doing business with another company because its employees are nonunion would be a violation of the section.

The agreement between the union and the company does not have to be in writing and it may be implied.

What Do You Do if Your Business Is Subject to a Union Organizing Drive

Generally speaking, union organizing drives are either internally or externally generated. Internal drives are ones where an employee or group of employees contact a union for help in organizing the workforce. The union at that time will evaluate the situation and give the employees assistance on how to organize. An external drive is one where the union targets a particular employer. This might happen for a variety of reasons, which could include articles about the employer in a local newspaper noting the company's profitability. It might be due to a directive from the local union's higher headquarters to organize in a particular industry. It might be due to the union reading about a merger or acquisition that affects the company. Union's know that employees are often feeling vulnerable during such times. Regardless of whether the drive is internal or external, the following rules and pointers are applicable.

Early Warning Signs

The last thing you as an employer want to do is to respond to a union-organizing drive that is not there. This is so for several obvious reasons. First, it may generate interest in a union among employees when there is none to begin with. Second, you may unnecessarily give a few malcontents the opportunity to level unfair labor practice charges against you for no reason. Third, it is a waste of your time to respond to a problem that does not exist.

Probably the most telling early warning sign is unusual behavior among employees. Only you know what is usual and what is not. Some employees bicker and argue among themselves all of the time. That is not a sign of union activity. However, if employees who are normally calm start to argue, or if employees who often argue become silent, this could be a sign that something is afoot. This "something" may not necessarily be a union—but, it could be.

As a supervisor, you probably know which employees are friends with each other, and which employees don't like each other. If those friendships seem to be getting strained, or if formerly unfriendly employees become friendly, this could be a sign that it is opinions about a union that are driving their behavior.

Unusual or suspicious congregations of employees also could be a sign, especially if it appears that one of them has been appointed a "lookout" in case management personnel approach. If they stop talking when you come near, you just might have broken up an impromptu union meeting.

Frequent use of the restroom facilities by employees may be a sign. It has been said that more union organizing has occurred in employer restrooms than in all of the union halls of the world. Whether this is true or not, employees frequently meet in such places to plan or discuss organizing.

The presence of union literature (brochures, flyers, etc.) is usually a sure sign of union activity. These will often be left in break rooms and restrooms. They also may be found in the parking lot or on employee desks.

Employees' use of language that sounds like what a union organizer might use is often a sign. For example, employees all of the sudden talking about "just cause" to discharge someone, seniority "rights," strikes or "job actions," shop stewards, and the like. Employees often go to union meetings or read union literature and pick up terms such as these. Related to this is the phenomenon of employees coming to you and other supervisors and asking what appear to be "loaded" or "planted" questions. For instance, an employee who comes and asks you if you believe you have to have just cause to discharge someone or whether you got a share of the company's profits for last year. Of course, if employees have always asked these types of questions, it is nothing. But, if it starts suddenly, you may have a union drive in progress.

Strangers on or near the facility may be a sign that something is going on. Many full-time union organizers (as opposed to employee organizers) will stand outside the entrance to your facility and hand out flyers or union cards (we will talk later about union cards) or otherwise attempt to communicate with your employees. Some organizers are even bolder and will venture onto your property (usually parking lots) and hand out union literature and try to talk with employees. Usually, this occurs at the beginning and end of the work day or at shift change. Sometimes the organizers may appear at the lunch hour.

Occasionally, unions will send surveys to your company asking about your wage rates, number of employees, benefits, and other information. Rarely will the union identify itself as the author of the survey. Instead, it will appear to come from some agency or community organization. Of course, your company will not answer such surveys, but it may be a sign that you are being targeted.

Although there may not be a sign of union activity at your facility, if there is union activity in the "neighborhood" you might want to be extra vigilant. Often such activity will spill over into your workplace. Similarly, if you know that your vendors and suppliers are unionized, these employees sometimes spread the union message to your own people. If a vendor's workforce is itself in the process of being organized, the likelihood of the vendor's employees "talking up" the union to your employees is high.

One of the best ways to detect these "signs" early on is to stay in touch with your employees. Be visible and accessible. Don't stay in your office, but get out "amongst them." Develop a rapport with your employees. Let them know they can come to you with problems or concerns. If you do this, you will learn of the organizing drive much earlier.

The Do's and Don'ts

Once you have determined that a union organizing drive is present, what do you do? What shouldn't you do? Should you do anything at all? After all, isn't it up to the employees to determine whether they should form a union?

Whether to do anything at all is a policy decision, which will probably be made at the highest levels of the company.

Sometimes, it is best to do nothing at all because the union drive is too weak and is not going anywhere. If it appears that less than 5 percent or so of the employees actually support the union and are responding positively to the union's message, it may be best to let the drive die out on its own. Once again, why respond to the drive and risk generating interest in a dying effort? This is not to say, however, that you also ignore what is going on in the facility. Lack of response is not tantamount to ignoring the situation. Even though the drive may be on a downhill spiral, it could pick up momentum and become more of a concern. Further, you may just think it is dying out and it really is not. Any union drive has the potential to be successful.

Sometimes a company does nothing in response to a drive because that is its philosophy or because it has previously agreed with the union involved to remain "neutral" during an organizing drive. Certain public sector employers are banned by law from speaking out against a union drive.

Often unions complain that employers should allow employees to make up their own minds without interference from the employer. They argue that employees have rights under Section 7 of the Act to either support or not to support the union. It's their decision.

This argument might make some sense if the union also was not communicating with the employees about the pros and cons of being in a union. This, however, never happens. The union always communicates to employees what advantages they will obtain with union representation. The union almost never tells employees any of the disadvantages or drawbacks of labor organizations. Thus, much like a political campaign, the voters (in this case, the employees) are best served if they hear both "sides of the story."

Thus, you are not being "antiunion" just because you tell employees what the disadvantages are of unionization, no more than the union is being "antiemployer" by telling employees of the benefits labor unions offer. There are pros and cons "both ways."

You need to know that, if your company does want to oppose the union drive, the drive is most vulnerable to defeat in its early stages. Thus, the earlier you detect and respond to a union drive, the better your odds of being successful in stopping it. If you don't find out about the drive or respond until the union has petitioned the Labor Board for an election, you may be too late.

What You Can't Do

There is much more that you *can* do compared to what you *can't* do ... so, let's start with the can'ts."

You can't threaten, either explicitly or by implication. You cannot walk up to an employee organizer and threaten to fire him if he does not abandon the union. You cannot threaten that the plant will close down if the union is voted in. You cannot tell employees that you will make their lives miserable if they support the union. You cannot hint that you will retaliate against employees if they support the union or if the union is voted in. Obviously, if you not only threaten, but also carry out such threats, by firing union supporters, etc., you will be in violation of the law.

Related to the above is making statements to the effect that selecting the union would be a futile gesture for the employees. Statements, such as "we will never bargain with the union if they are elected" or "you will never get a contract if the union wins the election," are examples of this.

You can't bribe employees to support the company or abandon the union. It is unlawful to promise to give employees wage raises or promotions if they abandon their support for the union or vote against the union.

It does not matter whether the employee is or is not a union supporter. You cannot bribe him or her to do anything against the union. For instance, if you were to promise a day off to an employee you knew to be antiunion if he went out in the workplace and spoke against the union, this would be against the law.

A common example is where the employer knows employees are organizing a union because they are dissatisfied with wages or maybe they don't like a particular supervisor. It would be illegal to promise employees you will raise their wages or fire the supervisor in order to persuade them to abandon the union. This seems to defy common sense. Why would you not want to remedy the problems that are causing the employees to support the union? Unfortunately, the time to remedy problems is *before* the union campaign starts, not afterwards.

You cannot interrogate employees about the union or about their beliefs regarding the union. As a supervisor, and a representative of the company, you are naturally curious as to how many employees support the union, why the union is organizing the plant, why employees favor the union, which ones do not favor the union, etc. Unfortunately, you will have to get these answers by some means other than by asking your employees. It is unlawful to interrogate employees about their union beliefs or union activities. Also, it is unlawful to interrogate them about the union beliefs and activities of others.

It is not unlawful, however, to listen if employees come to you (voluntarily) and volunteer information. Be careful, however, on asking questions in response to what they tell you. It is usually best just to take the information, thank the employee, and leave it at that. Naturally, this information may (and should) be shared with your superiors and other supervisors.

You cannot spy on employees union activities or give the impression that you are. You are curious to know how many people are attending a union meeting at the union hall a few miles from the plant. So you drive there and park across the street and count employees going into the meeting. Or maybe you take down the license plate numbers of the cars in the lot so you can ask your friend in the state highway patrol to check on the registration of the cars. What better way to see who is supporting the union? All of this, however, is unlawful. You cannot place union supporters or union organizers under surveillance.

Sometimes questions arise about video cameras and the like. Certainly, if the video cameras are already up before you learn about the organizing drive, it would be hard to successfully claim you were violating the law by continuing to use the cameras. If you install them after the drive begins, however, a persuasive case might be made that you are doing so to spy on union activity.

You also are prohibited from giving the impression that you are (or have been) spying on the union. For instance, you cannot go up to an employee and tell him that you know who the union ringleaders are or that you know how many employees were at the union meeting last night (even though you really don't know).

You cannot discriminate against an employee because of his or her union activities, nor can you favor an employee because he/she is against the union. You probably recall the discussion of employer unfair labor practices involving discrimination against employees for exercising their rights under Section 7. This unfair labor practice is found in Section 8(a)(3). Much of that discussion applies here. If it appears that you are singling out union adherents for unfavorable treatment, the election could be set aside. Similarly, if you are favoring those who oppose the union, you could run afoul of the law. You must be able to justify your actions, especially when a union organizing drive is afoot. You must be careful to follow company policy and to treat like cases alike. This is the best way to avoid a discrimination charge. Documentation of progressive discipline is crucial here. If you cannot document that you warned someone, in the eyes of the Board, it never happened. Just make sure you have good, legitimate business reasons for taking action. Ask yourself, "Would I be doing the same thing if this person were not a union supporter?" If your answer is "no," you are in a danger zone and should reconsider your actions.

What You Can Do

In most circumstances, you *can* do or say anything that is not prohibited in the Can't Do section above. That doesn't mean you *should* do it, merely that it is not unlawful. What you should say and do will largely depend on the union you are dealing with, the issues that they are discussing with your employees, the history of the company in dealing with its employees, and a host of other factors. What follows are some of the more common things supervisors say to their employees when they discover that a union drive is afoot.

You can tell employees about the implications of signing a union authorization card. When you first learn that a union is organizing your employees, one of the things the union is undoubtedly doing is asking employees to sign what is known as an authorization card. (See Appendix 6 for a sample.) These are usually postcard-sized documents that contain a statement to the effect that the signer of the card wants the union in question to represent him or her for purposes of collective bargaining. The card will have blanks for the employee to fill out his or her name as well as other information that might include phone number, address, job classification, and shift.

Under the law, if at least 30 percent of the employees in the bargaining unit (a term that will be explained later in more detail) sign a card, the union may file a petition with the NLRB to hold an election. Because the union needs a majority of those who vote in an election to actually win, however, many unions will often wait until they have cards from 65 to 70 percent (or even more) of the employees before they file the petition.

The union, once they have cards from a majority of employees in the unit, may demand that the employer bargain with the union without an election ever being held. Most employers refuse this demand and also refuse to look at the cards that may be presented by the union business agent or other representative. The reason for this is that we do not know what the union agent told employees to persuade them to sign cards or if they even told employees what the purpose of the card is. There have been examples of where the union agent told employees that if they signed a card it was to just get on a mailing list, or to ensure that they would be invited to the next union meeting. In other words, the employees were not really informed of the true purpose of the card and, therefore, employers refuse to recognize the cards as a true indicator that a majority of employees support the union. Likewise, employees sometimes are actually coerced into signing a card, most often by their fellow employees. This is not to say that all unions (or even most of them) engage in such activities. The issue is that we never really know for sure what an employee was told and that a secret ballot election is usually a better way to determine employees' true choice, just like it is the favored method of deciding political contests or school bond elections.

If you become aware of the union drive early enough, chances are that many employees have not signed cards. This is the time to educate them about what signing a card really means and that signing a card could be the first step on a journey the result of which no one can predict and which could be unpleasant for company and employee alike. **Union organization drives are most vulnerable in the card-signing phase. The best time to stop the drive is at this juncture. If the union cannot get at least 30 percent of employees to sign cards, there will not be an election and, many times, the union just "goes away."**

Employees often ask how they may get their cards back once they sign them. Although you may not solicit employees to ask to get their cards back, you may certainly respond to questions about this subject. Technically, the employee should write the union or the NLRB and revoke their signature. In practice, this almost never works, but it may be of benefit to the employee and the company to let the union know they no longer have that employee's support.

Generally speaking, you should tell employees that they should get *all* of the facts before signing a card; they should hear both sides, not just what the union is telling them. It is sometimes useful to liken the situation to a political election. Very few intelligent people would vote for a candidate based merely on what that candidate said he or she would do. Most of us look at both (or all) candidates and compare what they say, how they say it, and whether what they say makes sense. We even consider what one candidate says about the other one, although sometimes with the proverbial "grain of salt." A union drive is no different.

You can tell employees how you feel about the union and your opinions about unions in general. Section 8(c) of the Act is known as the "free speech proviso." It allows the company to voice its opinions and views so long as they do not contain threats of reprisal or force, or promises of benefits. Thus, it is not unlawful for you to tell an employee that the company is not in favor of unions because they can create dissension or that you think unions are not in the best interest of the employees. Be ready, however, to back up your opinions with reasons, which do not constitute a threat or bribe. For instance, if you said that a union would not be in the best interests of employees because the company will close the plant if a union is elected, such would be an unfair labor practice. This statement, although couched in the form of an opinion, contains a threat.

Similarly, you should have good, solid reasons to back up your opinions. Employees are quick to sense exaggerations and falsehoods. They also are quick to spot faulty reasoning. Think about what you say. Think about it from the *employees'* perspective. What may sound good to you, may sound like "hogwash" to them.

This being said, there are very few limits to what you can say as long as you stay within the parameters for Section 8(c) and avoid the unfair labor practices discussed above. Many employers, for instance, when confronted with a union drive, educate employees about how unions work, what their officers earn, what the union's income is, and where most of it goes. They do this to back up their opinions that the union is a big business and not really interested in the employee except as a source of income. Now, this may or may not be a valid opinion (it might depend on the union or the local involved), but it is a common theme of many organizational campaigns.

It is also lawful to point out to employees what the union charges in dues and to express an opinion as to whether the employee receives a fair return on such payments.

There is a public document that will tell you a great deal about union finances, both at the international and local level. This document is called the LM-2 and may be obtained from the U.S. Department of Labor. Depending on which one you want, the document may also be available online (see Appendix 2 for the Web site).

Some employers use these documents (or even post them) to demonstrate that unions really are businesses. Additionally, the LM-2 will show that—at least with most unions—**most of their income is from dues and most of their expenditures is for salaries and expenses of officers and employees of the union**. This simple fact is often an "eye opener" for employees who think that the union organizer is performing something akin to a charitable act and is only trying to help the employees. While it is true the organizer may be out to improve the employees' lot in the workplace, that is rarely the organizer's only—or even principal—motive.

You can tell employees about your own experiences with unions or about the experience that other companies have had with unions. You may have worked in a company before that had a union. You may have dealt with a union as a supervisor of unionized employees or as a union member yourself. It is certainly permissible to tell employees of these experiences; just don't make a prediction that the same things will happen at this company. For instance, suppose you worked at a company whose employees were unionized and the plant closed due to economic difficulties. It would be permissible for you to point this out to employees and comment that the union certainly did not protect their job security. It would not be allowable, however, for you to say "the same thing will happen here if you vote the union in." That would be a threat.

Similarly, you may have been a union member and been called out on strike when you did not really want to do this. It might have made it difficult for you to support your family and you may have observed acts of violence or, at the least, bitter relations between company and employees. It would be lawful for you to tell your employees about such an experience and point out that strikes and all that goes with them are always a possibility when a union is in the picture. It would not, however, be allowable for you to say that a strike is likely to take place if the union is voted in.

You also may know of other companies in the area who have experienced labor disputes, perhaps even with the same union that is organizing your employees. Once again, it is permissible for you to share this information with your employees, but may not predict that the same thing will happen at your company.

Basically, you are merely telling employees that these are the things that happened to the other company when they voted in the union.

You can tell employees about union disciplinary proceedings, fines, and assessments. A little known aspect of belonging to a union is the possibility of union fines and disciplinary proceedings. Almost all unions, at the local and international levels, have procedures to deal with employees who, in the opinion of the union, do something detrimental to the union. This might be turning the union in to law enforcement or testifying against a fellow union member at an arbitration hearing. It could be crossing a picket line because the person had to work to support his or her family. It could be "conduct unbecoming a union member" or something similar.

Although such proceedings are governed by law, the protections afforded to the individual union member are minimal, at best. Basically, the person gets to know the charges against him or her, the right to defend himself at a union "trial," and the right to confront accusers. There is no right to have a lawyer present.

Such trials can result in fines and expulsion. The fines are enforceable in the courts of most states.

These procedures may be found in the constitutions and by-laws of most unions. Although unions claim to be democratic institutions—and most are—their disciplinary procedures leave something to be desired when it comes to fair play and due process. Employees can be told about these things during an organizing drive. Sometimes, it is useful to reprint the disciplinary sections of the by-laws and constitutions and distribute them to the employees.

You can tell employees how much their dues will be and for what those dues will be used. You can tell them about the possibility of dues increases or special assessments. Usually, the LM-2 document will reveal what the union's dues are. Be careful that you read the document correctly because some unions have dues structures that vary according to the type of employment. The worst thing you could do is to misquote the union's dues. In addition to dues, there are initiation fees. In the case of most new bargaining units, the union will waive initiation fees for all "charter" members of the bargaining unit.

From time to time, the union may have special assessments for different reasons. Some unions have an assessment to pay for legal representation of an employee at an arbitration proceeding or for some other "one time" event. Employees may agree or disagree with the purpose of the assessment. They will probably have to pay, however.

Unions often use part of their dues receipts for political, social, or other purposes, which are not directly related to their functions as bargaining representative. Unions are required to make annual disclosures of the portion of the dues going to such nonrepresentational activities. Theoretically, employees are given the right to object to the use of that portion of their dues and have such refunded. These are known as "Beck Rights," after a Supreme Court decision in 1988.* There is, in

---

* Communication Workers of America v. Beck, 487 U.S. 735 (1988) (cert. denied 487 U.S. 1233 (1988)).

reality, however, substantial pressure on employees in many unions not to file such objections. Sometimes this pressure is subtle, sometimes it is not. In all cases, however, it is up to the employee to object. Not all employees are willing to do this.

A union also has the right to raise its dues. In order to do so, it must give employees notice and an opportunity to vote, in one form or fashion. In other words, the dues the employees pay when they are first organized may be increased.

You can tell them about the company's position regarding unions. Believe it or not, some employees may be unsure how the company views unions. They may think the company does not care whether they vote in a union or whether they have to operate under a union contract. You need to make sure there is no misunderstanding about this basic issue.

It is well within the bounds of the law to tell employees that the company is opposed to unionization, although you should couple that with a statement that employees have the legal right to choose a union if they want. You can tell employees that the company believes it is in the best interests of the company *and* its employees to remain union free. Many companies believe that a union comes between it and its people and that the union could have a negative impact on the company's flexibility to run its business efficiently. This could have an adverse impact on all concerned. It is permissible to tell employees all of these things.

You can tell employees about the realities of collective bargaining. When a union wins an election, the only right it wins is the right to *bargain* with the employer for a contract. This stems from the employer's obligation to negotiate with the newly elected union. Notice, this does not mean a union is entitled to a contract, to any particular kind of contract, or to any particular level of pay or benefits in the contract. Much like other situations in life, a union gets only what it can negotiate. Many employees have not thought about this. Instead, they believe that electing a union will result in better wages and benefits and greater job security. This is so because this is what the union organizers have told them.

While it is undoubtedly true that many union contracts do contain wage and benefit enhancements for employees, there is no law that requires this. Further, many unions must sacrifice the interests of some employees in order to serve the interests of others in the context of negotiations. For instance, younger employees may want the union to negotiate higher hourly wages. Older employees may be more concerned about better health insurance or pension benefits. What happens if the union cannot make gains in all of these areas because they do not have the bargaining power to do so? What if the company is willing to give the union a concession in one of these areas only if the union gives the company a concession in another area? Who wins and who loses? These are things that may be shared with employees.

Bargaining for a labor contract is indeed a two-way street like most other negotiations. Typically, it is not an occasion where the union sits down with the company and dictates what must be in the contract. Usually, the company does not dictate the terms either.

Another aspect of collective bargaining that may surprise some employees is the length of time it can take to negotiate a first contract. Many employees believe that the fruits of "being union" fall from the tree into their hands shortly after the election. This is usually not the case.

Typically, both sides are somewhat distrustful of each other after an election. Harsh words may have been exchanged in the campaign leading up to the vote. It takes a while sometimes to get the bargaining process going. Secondly, the entire contract must be negotiated from scratch. Unlike negotiations for a renewal contract, where many of the clauses remain unchanged, a first contract involves the creation of an entire document from A to Z. Third, there will be considerable wrangling over wages and benefits in many first contract situations. The company understandably feels that it has been providing a fair economic package. The union, on the other hand, must live up to its campaign promises to better the lot of its new members.

It is not unusual for it to take over a year to negotiate a first contract. Employees need to know that they will not get "immediate gratification."

It is useful as well to point out to employees the uncertainty of the outcome of negotiations. Truthfully, no one knows how it will come out. Will employees get less or more? Will they gain in some areas and suffer in others? Will there be an agreement at all? What happens if there is no agreement? How long will the process take? Will one group of employees benefit over another? The list could go on and on. The point is that entering into collective negotiations begins a journey fraught with uncertainty and doubt. It may come out okay and then, it may not. *Never predict loss of benefits, strikes, or other negative outcomes. Merely note that these are possibilities, among many other possibilities.*

You can explain to employees what happens if there is a deadlock in negotiations. The legal term for this is *impasse*. If the parties are at impasse, the duty to continue bargaining is suspended (unless and until the impasse is later broken, such as by one side backing down or significantly changing its position on an item that has caused the impasse). The employer may implement the terms of its final proposal at impasse. What are the union's options at this point? Basically, they are either to have its members work under the terms of the imposed final proposal or to strike.

If there is a strike, employees will have to choose whether they will work or participate in the strike. They have the right under Section 7 of the Act to choose. If they cross the picket line, they will be subject to expulsion, fines, or other discipline by the union. They could be subject to threats against themselves and their families. Who knows whether any of these threats will be carried out. They certainly will be subject to criticism of the harshest kind from their striking co-workers and be called a "scab."

If, on the other hand, the employee chooses to strike, he or she will not be receiving pay from the employer. Benefits could be cut off as well, including health insurance for the worker and family. Most states do not allow striking employees to obtain unemployment compensation benefits. Beyond this, union strike funds often do not cover newly organized employees and, even if they do, the payment from the union is often a pittance and not enough to buy the most basic necessities of life.

This is not a pretty picture. Whether to strike or not is a hard choice. You may remind employees that—if there is no union in the picture—they will never be put to that choice.

You can challenge union "promises." While it is unlawful for the employer to promise benefits, wage hikes, and the like, a union freely may make "promises" of this sort. It is not at all unusual for unions to tell employees in the midst of a campaign that they will get them "free" health insurance or a certain amount of wage increase. It unlawful for the employer to make similar promises because, in the eyes of the NLRB, the employer actually has the power to make its promises come true. The union does not. The NLRB believes employees know this, but my experience often has been just the opposite.

If the union makes promises of this nature, you may tell employees that the union organizers have no idea of what, if anything, they can deliver. We have already discussed the process of collective bargaining. What the final contract will look like—as we know—is anything but certain.

Ask employees how someone can make a promise about the outcome of a process that is like diving into muddy water. You don't know what's underneath.

Many times unions will claim that they can provide "job security" to employees. This sounds good to the average worker. Who doesn't want security in their lives? The problem is that employees do not often think too deeply about these promises; most of us do not overanalyze the good things we hear; we want to believe them so badly. You may ask employees to think about what job security really is. Who can guarantee job security? There are hundreds of examples of unionized operations going bankrupt or laying off large numbers of bargaining unit members. Did the unions involved in these companies somehow fail in their duty to maintain job security for their members? The answer is neither yes or no. The answer is that the union has nothing to do with job security.

In a capitalist society, especially in the private sector of our economy, there is no such thing as a guaranteed job. The "job security" of workers is directly tied to the financial well being of the company for which they work. The financial well being of the company is dictated by a host of factors, such as customer satisfaction, marketing, product quality, leadership, efficiency, productivity, competition, investment in capital equipment, location, price and availability of raw materials, technology, etc. Unions have no control over these things in any given company. It follows, therefore, that they have no control over job security.

When one stops to think about it, the closest we can come to having job security is for each employee to do his/her job to the best of his/her ability and to provide customers with a good quality product or service at a fair, competitive price. Once again, unions have nothing to do with this.

Unions may claim that they offer protection against unfair discipline or discharge. Perhaps this is the kind of "job security" they are touting in your case.

It is true that unions usually negotiate contractual provisions that require discipline and discharge to be for "just cause." Other provisions of the contract typically provide for a grievance procedure that ends in binding arbitration by a neutral third party if the parties cannot resolve the dispute themselves.

Most of the grounds for discipline or discharge under a union contract are the same as those found in policy manuals of union-free employers. If the employer has a good case against the employee, in all probability the employer's action will be upheld. Beyond this, the union is not automatically bound to take each case to arbitration. It may decide that some cases do not merit arbitration. As long as it exercises its discretion in a nonarbitrary manner, the employee has no recourse.

Sometimes unions trumpet their ability to exert control in the workplace to stop unfair actions by supervisors and the like. The truth of the matter is that unions have very little control over the day-to-day workings of the company. They also have little control over major corporate decisions that have an impact on workers lives, such as subcontracting, plant closures, layoffs, etc. To the extent that such items are influenced by the union depends on whether the union can negotiate them in the contract. Many companies are unwilling to surrender rights in these basic areas. Under the law, they do not have to. Why should they? In fact, most labor contracts contain what is known as a "management rights clause," which reserves to management the ability to run the company pretty much as it did before the union came along. Here is an example:

> The Company retains the exclusive right to manage the business. All rights, powers, functions and authority of the Company that it had prior to the time any Union became certified as exclusive bargaining representative of employees of the company and which are not explicitly abridged by a specific provision of this Agreement, are retained by the Company. Among the rights, which the Company specifically retains, are the rights to establish rules of conduct; to plan, direct, and control operations; to schedule and assign work to employees; to determine the means, methods, processes, and schedules of operation; subcontract or contract-out all or any part of the work that may be performed either more economically or expeditiously or for any other reason deemed sufficient by the Company; to establish standards and to maintain the standards and to maintain the efficiency of employees; to establish and require employees to observe Company rules and regulations; to hire, lay off, or relieve employees from their duties for lack of work or other legitimate reasons; and to maintain order and to suspend, promote, demote, discipline, and discharge employees for just cause. The Company also retains the right to close all or a portion of the facilities covered by this Agreement or to sell, relocate, or in any way to dispose of or convert such facilities.

> The exercise of any right enumerated in this Article, herein shall not be considered or construed as a violation of the Agreement, or in violation of any rights possessed by the Union or by bargaining unit employees.

I have been involved in several union campaigns where the company showed similar clauses to employees to dispel the union's inflated claims of its ability to influence the workplace.

You can point out to employees that the union is a business and why it needs their votes. We have already learned about the LM-2 form that shows the union's finances and the salaries of its officers. The main lesson we learn from studying such documents is that the union is a business. Like any other business, it needs income. To get income it needs customers (members). The more members it has, the more income it will receive because members pay dues and are subject to assessments.

Unions are as different, one from another, as are people. Two locals of the same union, moreover, may be entirely different in their methods and goals. Some unions are genuinely concerned about employees and others are not as concerned. Regardless of these differences, there is one common denominator: unions are businesses and are operated as such.

There is nothing wrong with this except that employees often do not understand it. Employees sometimes think that the organizer is like someone from the Red Cross or Salvation Army who just wants to help them. Employees need to know that, when the union organizes a new group of workers, it is merely marketing its service to potential customers. This is a process the union undertakes not out of a sense of charity, but out of business necessity.

Remember, most of the union's income is derived from dues and most of its expenditures are for salaries of its own employees and officers. Many of these people are handsomely compensated. As noted elsewhere, all of this is public knowledge and may be shared with employees.

You can tell employees about compulsory union membership. Most all unions—except in Right to Work states—will insist on having a union security clause in the contract. Such clauses require each employee in the bargaining unit to become a union member within a certain period of time following execution of the contract or, in the case of future employees, within a certain period of time of employment. The period often coincides with the probationary period. If the employee fails to become a member or maintain his or her membership in good standing, the union can require the employer to fire the employee.

The use of the word "member in good standing" is somewhat misleading in this context. In order to be in "good standing," all the employee must do is pay regular dues and assessments. He/she does not have to go to meetings, participate in union activities, or support union political and social causes.

Compulsory union membership is only possible in a state that has not enacted a Right to Work law. Beyond this, even in states that do not have Right to Work laws, there must be a union security clause in the contract between company and union before compulsory membership is permitted.

As noted above, however, unions almost always are able to negotiate a union security clause. They view this as necessary to maintain solidarity and to ensure an adequate return on their "investment" in organizing the workforce and administering the labor agreement.

The employee covered by a union security clause will be required to pay regular dues and assessments. Usually, these are deducted directly from the employee's check because the union also will negotiate a clause requiring the employer to make such deductions (a "check off" clause). Even in a Right to Work state, it is permissible for the company and the union to negotiate a check-off clause.

Both in a Right to Work state and in a non-Right to Work state, the employer must have a written authorization from the employee to deduct dues. All check-off clauses I have read require it and it is required by federal law and the laws of most states as well. The law also requires that the employee be able to revoke this authorization. The problem is that the employee cannot revoke the authorization anytime he or she feels like it. Usually, the authorization can be revoked only during a specified "window" period (a few days or a couple of weeks), usually on the anniversary of its signing. The authorization is a contractual document and its terms must be honored. Thus, even in a Right to Work state, if the employee signs a dues authorization, as a general rule, he/she will be required to stay with it for a year.

You can tell employees that the local union is often controlled by its parent (national or international) union and/or by regional offices. As noted above, unions are different, one from another. Almost all unions, however, are structured in a hierarchy. At the bottom of the chain is the local union. The local is the organization with which the employee will have the most contact. In most cases, locals are grouped together in regions or districts. Each region or district has its own leaders and staff. Essentially, the officials of the local answer to the leaders of the district or region. The regions or districts, in turn, report to the national headquarters of the union.

The control exercised by the top of the structure over the bottom varies from union to union. In some cases, the local is restricted from taking certain actions (such as strikes, raising dues, or executing a contract) without approval from "higher headquarters." At times, the priorities of the headquarters and the rank and file members in the local can differ significantly. Ordinarily, the local loses in any such conflict.

You can tell employees that unions often must choose between different groups of employees, deciding to favor one over another. As in many organizations, the local union is composed of a diverse group of people; diverse in terms of age, race, seniority, sex, political beliefs, and the like. These people have different needs and preferences. When it comes to negotiating a collective bargaining agreement, the union might not be able to accommodate all of these varied needs. For instance, the more senior people would be more interested in a rich retirement benefit. The younger workers, perhaps with children at home, want more in wages and are not concerned about retirement. Women might want liberal childcare leave provisions. Single, childless workers would not be too interested in such a benefit.

Ideally, the union would be able to obtain all of the above benefits in contract negotiations, i.e., something for everyone. In the real world, however, this is seldom possible. The union must make choices. Inevitably, such choices will alienate some of it members. How the union makes such choices varies from union to union and from situation to situation. The end result, however, is that the union may not always be able to uphold the interests of *all* of its members. Whether a given employee will be the beneficiary or the victim of this dynamic is anyone's guess.

You can tell employees that their dues may be used for political and social causes with which they do not agree. We have already discussed the fact the union dues are used for various causes that are not always directly related to the union's collective bargaining function. For instance, a well-known, union-supported group recently questioned the honesty and patriotism of a high ranking officer in the U.S. military who was involved in combat operations overseas. Many—including many union members—believed that the officer involved was unfairly treated. Unfortunately for many of them, their dues supported the offending organization.

Unions often target politicians who have not supported organized labor. Sometimes, union members may support these same politicians. Similarly, unions may support candidates who are not endorsed by many of their members.

How to Deal with the Union Business Agents

An initial clarification is in order here. When we use the term *union business agents*, we are speaking of outside union organizers or officials, not in-house employee organizers.

These people may contact you in person, by phone, by e-mail, or by regular mail. The purpose of their contact usually will be to announce they are organizing your employees or that they have already done so. They may ask you to look at a list of employees who have "signed up" or signed authorization cards. They may try to trick you into saying something that could be used against you later in an unfair labor practice proceeding. In short, they are not there to help you.

The first thing to realize (in the case of in-person visits) is that outside union officials have no right to be on company property. You should politely ask them to leave. If they do not, call law enforcement.

Second, despite your natural curiosity, do not look at any lists, cards, etc. This may make it difficult for the company to support any contention that it has a good faith doubt that the union is desired by a majority of your employees.

Third, do not get into any arguments with the union agents. This is exactly what they want you to do. Don't take the bait. Just tell them to leave.

Fourth, do not give out the names or contact information of anyone in the company. They will proceed to contact that person if you do. If they ask for such information, tell them that you will relay the request to the appropriate company official and, if deemed appropriate, the company will be in contact with them.

Finally, do not be tricked into admitting anything that could be construed as illegal. Union agents would love for you to say something such as, "We will never bargain with a union," or that "We will fire anyone who supports the union." Avoid answering any questions about company policy regarding unions or whether you will "respect the wishes of the employees" if they want a union. You are under no obligation to answer these questions or to engage in a debate. Nothing can be gained by arguing with the union agents and a lot could be lost by doing so.

When the union agent has left your office, immediately contact your supervisor and report the incident. Your company's legal department also may wish for you to prepare a document detailing what happened during the encounter.

How to Deal with Agents of the National Labor Relations Board

NLRB agents probably will not contact you during the organizing phase of the campaign until a petition is filed. We will deal with that later. The one exception to this would be if the union files an unfair labor practice charge. The contact will be by mail and followed up by a phone call. The mailing will contain the charge and a request for you to respond, in writing, by a certain date.

Shortly after the letter is sent, the Board agent will call a company official to determine if the company intends to respond to the charge and if it will make witnesses available for interview. It is usually best to tell the agent that the company will respond and that a decision will be made at a later date as to whether witnesses will be made available. It is advisable to ask the Board agent which witnesses he or she would like to interview. The content of the response and the decision on interviews should be made after receiving advice from legal counsel. You should not make this decision on the spot.

If the Board agent asks for phone numbers or other contact information regarding company officials, you should refrain from giving this information and, much as with the union business agent, tell the Board representative that some authorized official will respond.

Be cautious in dealing with NLRB agents. As the saying goes, anything you say can be used against you later. Nevertheless, most NLRB agents are true professionals and are merely trying to do their job. The company should cooperate fully in any investigation, but the decision on the content of the company's response should be made carefully.

The Uses and Abuses of No-Solicitation/No-Distribution Rules

If your company is targeted by a union organization drive, one of the most pressing problems you may have is to keep the work flow moving. For most companies, an organizing drive is a rare event. Employees are naturally curious and want to talk with their co-workers about it. Employees who are organizing for the union will want to solicit their fellow employees and distribute union literature and authorization cards. The most effective and convenient place for this activity is—in the eyes of the union supporters—the work place. True, the union may call meetings at its offices or some other location, but there is no way to compel employees to attend. At work, however, the audience will be much larger and attendance is guaranteed by employees' need to be at work.

On the other hand, the company has a strong interest in not allowing such activity to take place. This is so for two reasons: (1) it can interrupt work and (2) most companies oppose unions and do not want to make it convenient for their employees to organize.

Because the company owns the premises (or leases them), one might think that the company has the right to prohibit employees from advocating for the union while at work. However, this is not the law.

Nonemployee organizers

Let us first deal with the issue of organizers who are not employed by the company. These individuals are either on the union's payroll or are unionized employees of other companies who have volunteered to help their union organize your workplace.

These people may engage in a variety of activities including handing out leaflets in the parking lot, trying to meet employees who are outside the building taking a smoke break or eating lunch, or (especially in establishments open to the public) they may try to enter the workplace itself and speak with your employees. I can remember one occasion when the union agent visited my client, a grocery store, and distributed union literature on the premises and, before anyone reported it to management, had succeeded in disrupting the work of almost all employees and had been observed by several customers.

The important thing to remember about nonemployee organizers is that, unless you want them to be there, they are trespassers and should be asked to leave the premises. A "No Solicitation" sign on the outside of your property is recommended, but not required in order for you to enforce the company's rights in this regard. If the nonemployees refuse to leave, you may wish to call local law enforcement to enforce your property rights.

On the other hand, nonemployee organizers do have the right to be on public property to include sidewalks, etc. Unless they pose a traffic hazard, behave in a threatening or unlawful manner, or block entry or exit, there is not much that can be done. One "moral to the story" here: Know exactly where the property line of your business is located.

Employees

The U.S. Supreme Court decided many years ago that employees have greater rights than outside organizers when it comes to union solicitation and distribution of union literature.* In order to understand these rights and what limitation the employer can put on these rights, please keep the following terms in mind:

Working time: That part of the work day when employees are supposed to be at work. It does not include authorized break times, lunch period, or the time before and after the employee's work day. It also doesn't include time when an employee is unable to work (such as when his machine is broken down and is being repaired). This term should not be confused with "working hours" such as 8 to 5, which would include nonworking time as well as working time.

Working area: That part of the employer's facility where work is normally performed. It does not usually include lunch rooms, break rooms, or parking lots. These latter areas are referred to as "nonworking areas."

Solicitation: Means oral discussion between employees usually involving a situation where one employee is trying to persuade the other to support the union, but it could also include a discussion about the union. The handing out of authorization cards, although actually a document, is considered under the law to be a form of solicitation and dealt with under the rules pertaining to solicitation.

Distribution of Literature: Literature is sometimes referred to as "union propaganda," but this term is often unfair. Literature refers to flyers, handouts, booklets, and anything else of a similar nature. Often these documents are quite sophisticated and well-written. At other times, such documents are highly partisan and have an almost rabid tone. In any event, they are dealt with under a separate legal rule, as we shall see.

What follows is a discussion of how far an employer can go to prohibit union solicitation and distribution of literature. In reading these rules, remember this: AN EMPLOYER MUST HAVE ITS SOLICITATION/DISTRIBUTION OF LITERATURE POLICIES IN PLACE *BEFORE* THE UNION BEGINS ITS ORGANIZATION DRIVE. For instance, if you find out employees are passing out cards at work and then decide to write a policy, you are too late.

Does this mean that if you have no policy, you have to let employees do whatever they want to? The answer is no. You always have the right to instruct employees to work if whatever it is they are doing is interfering with their work. The value of having a policy is that it puts employees on notice as to the limits of their rights and also does not require you to wait until the activity is actually interfering with production to take action.

What can such policies prohibit and what must they allow to take place on our premises? Remember, the rules were crafted over the years to balance the employer's

---

* Republic Aviation Corp. v. NLRB, 324 U.S. 793 (1945).

right to run its business efficiently with the employees' rights under Section 7 to engage in concerted activity. Any "no solicitation" rule should be written and enforced with this balance in mind.

So, what are the rules? They include:

1. You may prohibit solicitation during working time in both working and non-working areas of the facility.
2. You may prohibit distribution of literature during working time in both working and nonworking areas of the facility. Additionally, you may prohibit distribution of literature in working areas of the facility even on nonworking time.

Located at Appendices 7 and 8 are charts that may help you understand these rules.

There are two other important things to know about enforcement of such rules.

First, both the employee doing the soliciting or distribution of literature and the employee being solicited (or participating in the discussion) and the employee receiving the literature must be on nonworking time in order to be able to solicit or distribute. For instance, if one employee is on break, but the other employee is on working time and he or she is soliciting the employee on break, the employee who is supposed to be working can be cautioned to get back to work or be disciplined, depending on the severity of the infraction and whether or not the employee has been warned in the past.

Second—and this is a very important part of the law in this area—you cannot enforce your policy only against solicitation and distribution related to union activities if you do not enforce it against other forms of such activity, e.g., Avon solicitation, solicitation to buy a car, etc. If you single out union activity, then you are discriminating against the union and have committed an unfair labor practice. Any employees fired or disciplined under such a discriminatory policy can be reinstated, given back pay, and have any record of discipline removed from their files.

Many employers allow employees to solicit and distribute literature during work time. Think about it. We allow employees to solicit other employees to buy used cars, Girl Scout cookies, and a host of other items. There is a recent Labor Board case (decided in 2007) that holds that if you only ban commercial solicitation then you can allow employees to conduct charitable solicitation without running afoul of the discrimination rule.* The policy in this case read:

> Company communication systems and the equipment used to operate the communication system are owned and provided by the Company to assist in conducting the business of The Register-Guard.

---

* The Guard Publishing Company, 351 NLRB No. 70 (2007).

Communications systems are not to be used to solicit or proselytize for commercial ventures, religious or political causes, outside organizations, or other nonjob-related solicitations.

In my opinion, this clause would be made even better by noting that nonjob-related solicitation would be allowed as long as they were not commercial in nature.

Thus, it is possible to draft a policy that will allow employees to solicit charitable, noncommercial organizations, such as the United Way or a school fundraiser (or sell their private vehicle), yet, at the same time, ban commercial solicitation for outside organizations, including Amway, Avon, cell phone cards, and unions.

There are two things to be noted at this point. First, as with all Board-created law, this case is subject to being overruled or modified. You should check with your legal advisor before implementing this type of policy. Second, when enforcing any no-solicitation policy, you need to be practical and fair. If two employees engage in a short conversation that does not interfere with work, you should not discipline them, even if it technically violates your no-solicitation policy. *The time to step in is if it interferes with work.* Punishing employees for talking about unions for a few seconds (but allowing them to talk about fishing for the same, brief amount of time) will only make you look bad and might get you into legal trouble. In my experience, no employer has successfully opposed union organization solely through enforcement of a no-solicitation rule. The best way to defeat a union organizing drive is to be fair, open, and unafraid to state your opinion in accordance with the rules given earlier in this book.

Authorization Cards

We have already discussed this subject above. Authorization cards are undoubtedly the most important tool in the union's organizing arsenal. If the union organizers succeed in obtaining the signatures of at least 30 percent of the employees in the bargaining unit (the group of employees that the union wants to organize), it may petition the Labor Board to hold a secret ballot election. If the union obtains signatures from a majority of employees in the bargaining unit, it may ask the employer to recognize the union voluntarily without an election ever being held. Under current law, the employer is under no obligation to do this and may require the union to file a petition for an election.

Most employers will demand that the union file a petition when confronted with a union claim that it represents a majority of employees in the proposed bargaining unit. This is so because it is often uncertain what employees have been told about the legal implications of signing a card. It also is possible that some employees have been coerced into signing. While this is not always true, it is impossible to know what employees were told by the union organizer or their co-workers when they signed the card.

If you are considering recognizing the union based on a card majority, you should have a neutral third party examine the cards and compare them to a known handwriting exemplar of the employee (such as his or her signature on tax forms on file with the employer). It is an unfair labor practice to recognize a union as the bargaining agent if it does not, in fact, represent a majority of employees.

As noted above, many times unions will not file a petition unless they have obtained signatures from 60 or 70 percent of the employees in the unit. This is because the union knows that there will often be a lessening of support between the time of the petition and the election, mainly due to the employer's antiunion campaign. Thus, as a general proposition, if you get a petition in the mail, or if the union demands recognition, you can assume that at least 60 percent of employees have signed cards—and perhaps even more.

The card itself is usually about the size of a post card. The language will vary with each union, but in essence the card contains a statement that the employee wishes the union to be his or her representative for purposes of collective bargaining. There is a place for a signature and date. Most cards also ask that the employee furnish other information that might include job title, shift, home phone number, and address.

As noted above, most employers refuse to examine the cards if they are going to insist the union file a petition with the Board.

How to Deal with Questions from Your Employees

We have discussed above the do's and don'ts as to communicating with employees. It is important to note at this point that the card signing phase is when a union organizing drive is at its most vulnerable. If you learn of a card signing campaign, it is often best to inform employees of the legal significance of signing a union card and the potential consequences. If employees ask you questions about this, you may inform them consistent with the rules we have set forth above.

Remember, it is best not to predict dire consequences. It is better to note the uncertainty that union organization may cause. Always tell your employees that the company will respect their rights under the law. If an employee asks a question to which you do not know the answer, tell him/her you will get back with him/her, get help, and follow up with the employee. If you are unsure, don't guess. Also, union organizers are sometimes not above feeding "trick" or "set up" questions to employees to ask their supervisors and hopefully elicit an answer that could be the basis of an unfair labor practice charge. If you think this is happening to you, just try to apply the rules you learned in this book. If this doesn't help, tell the employee you will get back with him/her and seek help. Try to keep your cool. Sometimes, union-oriented employees have been instructed how to provoke supervisors into getting angry and unlawfully threatening employees. **Remember**: It's always lawful to tell employees to get back to work.

Recognitional Picketing and How to Deal with It

Sometimes a union will set up a picket line at the company's facility to pressure the employer to recognize it. There are some important rules that you should know. First, such pickets—even if they are your off-duty employees—have no right to picket on company property. If they do, they should be asked to leave. If they do not leave, call law enforcement. Second, recognitional picketing can only take place for thirty days unless a petition for election is filed. If the picketing goes on beyond the thirty days and no petition has been filed, an unfair labor practice charge may be filed against the union.

Usually, the company will deal with such picketing through its legal counsel (which is advised). You may be called upon to monitor the picketing if it becomes violent or disrupts access to or from the facility. You also may be asked to monitor language on the picket signs to ensure it is consistent with a recognitional purpose.

The "Ins and Outs" of a Labor Election

The Petition

As discussed above, the petition for an election is based upon a sufficient number of employees signifying their desire for union representation, usually by signing authorization cards.

The petition itself is a one-page document that is filled out by the union or by the union with Board assistance. A sample petition may be found at Appendix 9. As you may see, it is a simple document, but a very important one.

The petition contains some useful information for the company. Mainly, it discloses the union involved and the group of employees the union seeks to represent (the bargaining unit). The petition also will disclose the number of employees the union *thinks* is in the bargaining unit. Sometimes they will be wrong and it will make a difference in whether they have enough authorization cards. In any event, the petition should be referred to the company's legal advisor to determine the most appropriate course of conduct to take.

With the petition will come a notice to employees that the Board asks be put in places where employee notices are commonly posted. The notice informs employees that a petition has been filed and advises them of their rights. Under current law, you are not required to post this notice. Many employers choose not to do so. Just because a petition has been filed does not necessarily mean that an election ultimately will be held. If you do choose to post the notice, ensure it is not defaced. If it is, request another one from the Board. To avoid this problem, consider posting the notice in a glass case.

The Board also will provide you with pamphlets describing the election process and employee rights. The Board asks that you reproduce and distribute these to employees. Once again, most employers choose not to do this.

The "Critical Period" Doctrine

Once a petition is on file, the Board views the time period between this event and the election as the "critical period." This means that any employer action against an employee will be scrutinized very closely if an unfair labor practice charge is filed. This is not the time to try to change policies, institute a no-solicitation rule, or try to redress old grievances. The time for that has passed. This is not to say you cannot run the company in an efficient manner. What you must do, however, is to be doubly sure that you can justify any discipline, demotions, or other changes that might adversely impact employees.

Both the Board and the union will be watching you once a petition is filed. This, of course, is another reason to defeat the campaign in its card-signing phase.

The Bargaining Unit

This is a very important concept to understand. The bargaining unit has two purposes:

1. It will be the group of employees eligible to vote in the election. Employees outside the bargaining unit have no voting rights in a labor election.
2. If the union wins the election, this will become the group of employees for whom the union will try to get a contract.

Under the National Labor Relations Act, the Labor Board is tasked with determining an appropriate bargaining unit if a petition is filed. Notice that the law does not say the Board must find *the most appropriate* bargaining unit. As such, the Board has wide discretion in determining what the bargaining unit should be.

What are the considerations the Board uses? We must know this in order to determine whether we will challenge the union's bargaining unit specified in its petition.

The Board uses what is known as a "community of interest" standard in deciding bargaining unit issues. A variety of factors are examined, but it all boils down to this: Does the group of employees in question have enough in common with each other that it makes sense to treat them as a unit or group for purposes of the election and collective bargaining.

Following are some of the factors examined by the Board:

- Geographical proximity: Does the employer have multiple sites? If so, it is likely that a single site will be an appropriate unit as opposed to the entire chain of facilities.
- Common supervision: If the production and maintenance employees are supervised by the same person, this makes it more likely that they have that commonality of interest.
- Employee interaction: If two groups of employees rarely have contact with each other, it is less likely that the Board would find sufficient community of interest to

group them together for purposes of collective bargaining. For instance, a group composed of secretaries and production workers probably would be found not to be an appropriate unit. If, on the other hand, there is interchange of employees (especially temporary transfers) between two groups of otherwise separate employees, the Board might find there to be sufficient community of interest. The idea here is that if employees go back and forth between two segments of the employer's workplace, they have more in common with each other.

- Job skills: The Board will look at the jobs the employees do in determining an appropriate unit. If the jobs require a similar amount of skill or training, the Board might group them together. On the other hand, if the jobs are entirely different, it is unlikely the Board will find a community of interest. An example of this would be a switchboard operator and a maintenance worker.
- The Board has special rules when the union wants to group skilled craftsmen with unskilled or semiskilled laborers. Typically, the skilled workers will have to vote in favor of inclusion. There is a similar rule for inclusion of professional employees, such as engineers with a group of nonprofessional employees.
- Guards may not be included in a bargaining unit with other employees.
- Integrated enterprises: If one part of a facility makes a part that is put together with parts made by another part of the facility, there is a community of interest. An example of this would be a department that makes airplane engines and a department that makes the fuselage of an airplane.
- The unit petitioned for by the union: Naturally, the unit that the union believes is appropriate is a factor the Board will consider, although it is not necessarily the controlling factor.
- Common personnel policies, centralized control of labor relations: Even in the case of a multisite employer, there have been cases where the Board has ruled that all sites must be included in the bargaining unit due to the fact that the employer's control of labor relations was highly centralized.
- Special Rules for Acute Care Hospitals: Because of the desire to promote smooth labor relations in such facilities, Congress enacted legislation in 1989 to control the number of bargaining unit possibilities in hospitals. The following units (or combination of units) are permissible:

> All registered nurses
> All physicians
> All professionals except for registered nurses and physicians
> All technical employees
> All skilled maintenance employees
> All business office clerical employees
> All guards
> All nonprofessional employees except for technical employees, skilled maintenance employees, business office clerical employees, and guards

One important thing to remember about bargaining unit determinations it that no one factor is controlling. In many cases, some factors point to one type of unit and other factors point to some different configuration. If the parties disagree on what unit is appropriate, it is up to the Board to decide and its decision is usually final.

Eligibility to Vote

Only employees in the bargaining unit will be eligible to vote. Supervisors are not eligible to vote under any circumstances. Employees must be on the payroll by a certain date to be eligible. This, not surprisingly, is referred to as the "payroll eligibility date." The Board will make this determination, but it is usually the end of the pay period immediately preceding the filing of the petition. The purpose behind this rule is to prevent the employer from hiring several employees after being served with a petition in an effort to dilute the union's support.

Employees must still be on the payroll on the date of the election in order to be eligible. There are some important exceptions to this rule. If an employee was fired and the union claims he/she was fired for union activity, that employee will vote a challenged ballot (to be explained later). Whether his/her vote counts will depend on the outcome of the charge and whether challenged votes could affect the outcome of the election. Many times, disputes over voter eligibility—particularly whether someone is a statutory supervisor—are decided in a proceeding known as a "representation hearing."

Representation Hearing

Most elections are decided without a representation hearing being conducted. This is because the parties agree on the bargaining unit, eligibility to vote, and other matters.

When a hearing is necessary, it is conducted before an employee of the Labor Board. Witnesses are sworn and evidence is taken although the overall process is informal. The hearing officer will make his or her recommendation to the regional director on how the dispute should be resolved. The decision of the regional director may, upon request of the aggrieved party (or both parties), be reviewed by the National Labor Relations Board.

As you may see, a representation hearing and its aftermath can slow the process considerably.

Because of the desire to avoid wrangling over representation hearing issues, the union and the Board will often entertain the employer's suggestion on the date of the election, the time the polls will be open, and where the election will be held. These can be important considerations.

Usually, the employer will want the election "pushed back" as far as possible in order to formulate its antiunion campaign and to give it sufficient time to persuade employees to change their minds about supporting a union. After all, just because an employee signed an authorization card does not mean that he/she must vote for the union in the election.

Many "old hands" in the labor relations business believe it is to the employers advantage to have the election on a payday, instead of on a day near the end of the pay period when a lot of employees may be "broke" and irritated that they do not make more money. Others believe that having it on a Friday—whether or not a payday—makes some sense because employees are likely to be in a better mood. On the other hand, Monday elections are not very good for most employers because the union will use the weekend to solicit support. Additionally, most employees are not in the best of moods on Monday.

The time the polls are open can be crucial. The employer (and the Board) want to maximize voter turnout. Thus, setting a time that is convenient for employees will be the best strategy. For example, opening the polls one-half hour before shift change and keeping them open one-half hour after shift change will maximize voter participation. At all costs, avoid times when employees must come to the facility from their homes in order to vote.

By the way, there is no such thing as an absentee ballot in a labor election. Employees on vacation or who are sick will not be able to participate in the election unless they personally appear to vote.

"Consent" versus "Stipulated" Elections

Not much time needs to be spent on this issue. A consent election is one where the regional director's decision will be final with respect to almost all issues that are disputed. Usually it is best not to opt for this form of election. The stipulated election will allow Board review of decisions of the regional director in the case of disputes.

The Excelsior List

After the election has been ordered by the regional director, he/she also will order the employer to produce a list of employees to the Board. This list will be sent to the union. This list is known as the "Excelsior List" and is named after an old Board case involving the Excelsior Underwear Company.* This document must contain an accurate alphabetical list of bargaining unit employees who were employed as of the payroll eligibility date or some other date set by the regional director. It is important that this list be accurate and furnished in a timely manner. The list must contain the full first and last name of the employee (no initials instead of a full first name) and the home address including zip code. The idea behind the list is for the union to have contact information on all bargaining unit employees. Because the employer already has this information and can always access employees at work, the Excelsior List is a way to level the playing field somewhat. Failure to furnish the

---

* Excelsior Underwear, 156 NLRB 1236 (1966).

list in a timely manner, inaccuracies, or omissions can result in an election being set aside by the Board upon the filing of an objection.

The "Big Blue Notice"

Once the regional director has directed that an election be held, the Board will furnish you with several copies of a large notice to be posted. This notice contains the particulars about the time and place of the election, a sample ballot, and a recitation of employee rights under the law. This notice is referred to as "Big Blue Notice" because of its size and the prominence of the color blue on the document. **This notice must be posted by the employer.** The notice should be posted in the place or places where notices to employees are usually posted. If the notice is defaced in any way (a popular thing for employees to do is to mark one of the boxes in the sample ballot, for instance), you should replace it immediately. Once again, consider putting the notice in a glass case, which can be locked. Failure to follow these rules can result in the election being set aside.

The Election Campaign

The Do's and Don'ts

Believe it or not, you already know most of these because they are the same rules as discussed above in the section "What Do You Do If Your Business Is Subject to a Union Organizing Drive," subsection "The Do's and Don'ts." Naturally, the statements about the dangers of signing an authorization card are moot, since, by this point, a majority of employees probably have signed the cards already.

One important thing to point out in relation to the cards, however, is the employees do not have to vote for the union just because they signed a card. Many employees do not understand this or they have been told that, if they sign a card, they are committed to vote for the union. Employees must be told that this is not true. Signing a card does *not* obligate them to vote for the union. Beyond this, in a secret ballot election, no one will know how they voted.

In my experience, the best antiunion campaign is for supervisors to talk with employees on a one-on-one basis. Don't haul the employees into your office. Just chat with them privately on the shop floor or a quiet part of the office. If you have rapport with your employees and deal with their concerns honestly, you have a better chance of convincing them that a union may not be in their best interests.

You must avoid, naturally, any threats either direct or indirect. You must not spy on employees or place them under surveillance. Open, frank communication is the best way to maximize a positive outcome. Go back and review the rules in the above section "What Do You Do If Your Business Is Subject to a Union Organizing Drive." Most all of these apply during an election.

Employer "Free Speech" Rights

We have already discussed Section 8(c) of the National Labor Relations Act that, in essence, allows employer representatives to voice their opinions about unions so long as such statements do not contain threats of reprisals or promises of benefits.

You have this right at all times, not just during an election campaign, but it is here that you will rely on it the most.

You should not be afraid to voice your opinion. You may speak of the union in unfavorable terms if you wish. Just remember, never underestimate the intelligence of your employees. Back up your opinions with facts. Be businesslike and avoid lecturing your employees. Do not overdo it. A word here and there will often be enough. Otherwise, you will appear to be obsessed by the union drive and employees will think you are frightened of the union. Also, remember that other representatives of the company will be taking part in the campaign. Don't think you have to take the "whole load" by yourself.

The Laboratory Conditions Standard

Although somewhat at odds with reality, the Board for many years has adhered to a Laboratory Conditions standard. What this means is that the Board wants conditions in the workplace prior to the vote to be as favorable as possible for employee free choice. The Board wants an atmosphere free of coercion by employer, union, or co-workers.

The important thing to note about this is that the Board could overturn the results of an election based on conduct that does not amount to an unfair labor practice. For instance, if the employer representative misled employees or lied to them about the union, this might not constitute an unfair labor practice. It might, however, violate the Laboratory Conditions standard leading the Board to overturn the results of an election should the union file objections. (We will discuss objections to an election later in this book.) This is yet another reason to be honest with employees and not resort to any "dirty tricks" to win the election. Not many things are worse than to win an election and then have it overturned because someone on the employer's side of the table got carried away.

Methods of Campaigning

One of the best methods, as noted above, is one-on-one meetings with supervisors or small group meetings. There are other methods, however. Speeches to large assemblies of employees are sometimes used. Letters to the employees' homes addressed to the employee and his/her family is another popular device. Postings on the bulletin Board and literature placed in the employees pay envelope (perhaps a dying method in these days of direct deposit) are both traditional methods to campaign.

I have found that sometimes the best ways to communicate with employees during a union campaign is to use existing forms of communication. For instance, if the employer has a weekly safety or information meeting, it is often a good idea to communicate the employer's message on these occasions. If a certain company official typically has been the one to give a speech to employees in the past, consider using that person in the union campaign. One of the worst things an employer can do is to bring in some highly placed company official to give a speech, someone who has never (or rarely) spoken to the employees before. Although there are exceptions to every rule, such actions usually provoke employee comments, such as "The only time Mr. X comes to talk to us is when he wants our vote," or something similar.

Some companies show employees videos depicting the disadvantages of unionization, sometime in very unflattering terms. Most of these videos, which can be purchased commercially, are lawful. There are a few, however, that have been held to have violated the Laboratory Conditions standard or constituted an unfair labor practice (usually in the form of a veiled threat). The company might wish to check with its legal advisor before showing such videos to its employees.

There are some other "gimmicks" used by management during a union campaign. A popular example of this is what is known as a "strike calculator." This device is similar to a paper slide rule and calculates how long an employee would have to work to break even if the union struck for a pay raise and got the raise, but only after a strike. Naturally, the length of time to reach the break even point will depend on the amount of the raise and the length of the strike. In most instances, the employee has to work quite a long while (perhaps a year or more) to make up for the lost income of a strike, even accounting for the pay raise.

Some companies distribute booklets to employees discussing the realities of unionization and the potential outcomes. If well written, these booklets are often effective. It is best, however, to seek legal advice before distributing any such booklet.

Captive Audience Speech

A "captive audience" speech is a speech given to a massed assembly of employees on company time and on company premises. Attendance is mandatory. Companies sometimes hold these speeches in the latter stages of the campaign. Another strategy is to save some of the most effective or damaging (to the union) campaign materials for use in this speech. Many people believe that, like a political election, you do not want to "peak" too soon. It gives the other side too much time for rebuttal. Colloquially, this concept is referred to as "shooting your big guns" at the very last. This may or may not be a wise campaign strategy. The answer depends on a variety of facts and circumstances. The point here is that it is often during the captive audience speech that these "big guns" are fired.

There are two things to remember about captive audience speeches. First, the same rules regarding do's and don'ts, laboratory conditions, and employer free speech, which we have discussed above, are equally applicable to that which is said during such speeches. Second, such speeches may *not* be given in the twenty-four-hour period immediately preceding the opening of the polls on election day. In other words, if the polls open at 2 p.m. on Friday, the company cannot give a captive audience speech unless it ends no later than 1:59 p.m. the previous day. It's best not to cut it too close here. This is another reason why you do not want a Monday election since the last opportunity many companies would have to hold the captive audience speech would be the previous Friday. This twenty-four-hour period is often referred to as the "insulated period."

Many people are confused with this rule and believe that *all* campaigning must cease during the insulated period. This is not true. Any form of campaigning may take place (subject to the electioneering rules discussed below) during the insulated period *except* a captive audience speech.

Common Union Strategies

Unions are as different as individuals. Even different locals within the same union sometimes have different ways to approach a campaign.

Nevertheless, there are several observations that can be made about union campaign strategy; just remember that these observations are generalities and will not hold true in every case.

First, many unions have abandoned the old blood and guts type of campaigning where they vilified the employer and cast the struggle as "us versus them" or otherwise promoted a class consciousness mentality. Many unions today are fairly businesslike in their approaches and will argue persuasively and logically to employees about the good a union can do for them.

Unions often argue that they bring justice to the workplace. That is, through the grievance and arbitration process, the rules of the labor contract will be enforced fairly and evenly. Unions often point out that this means the boss will no longer be able to "play favorites" or be arbitrary in handing out both punishments and rewards.

Unions point to certain statistics that unionized workers are better paid and enjoy better benefits than their nonunion counterparts. They note that this is why the employer is opposing the union, not because the company feels that the union will harm the employees, but because unionization causes a lessening of profits. There are many studies that bear out the above statements. There are others, however, that do not.

Job security is an important argument made by unions during election campaigns. Union's note that layoff procedures and discharge procedures are subject to the rules of the labor contract and legally enforceable. Senior employees especially will benefit from the layoff protections that usually require the employer to let go the junior employees first and recall in inverse order of seniority. Unions will contrast this to the power of a nonunion employer to lay off whoever it wants, even more senior employees, and who has no obligation to recall anyone (let alone in any particular order).

Unions will often tell employees that they will receive defined benefit pension plans and free health insurance, both through union programs. The fact that many of the union pension funds are in financial trouble is usually not mentioned.

Unions like to point out to employees that they are altruistic organizations (which is debatable) and interested in only the welfare of employees. They point to their long history of improving working conditions for the average American worker (which is true) to include the forty-hour work week, health insurance, and many other benefits that are taken for granted today. Unions argue that these improvements for the worker would not have been achieved (or would have been achieved much later) but for unions fighting for worker rights.

Unions will often hold meetings during the campaign. These meeting are held off the employer's premises. The union also may conduct mailing campaigns. As noted earlier, unions are allowed to visit employees in their homes to campaign. My experience is that most employees resent these intrusions and they are not much used any more.

Unions have become adept at using Internet and e-mail in their campaigns and an employer is well-advised to encompass these electronic forms of communication in its no-solicitation policies lest company computer equipment is hijacked by union supporters and used for organizational purposes.

Union supporters will often hand out leaflets or other literature. This may occur at work (subject, of course, to your rules). It also may occur in the parking lot. In some cases, a union organizer will stand outside the gate and hand out literature as employees are entering or leaving the facility.

Unions sometimes stage social events, such as picnics or dinners at a local restaurant to solicit support for their cause.

They may reach out to local community leaders who may be sympathetic to the union and enlist their support either by testimonials or by putting pressure on the employer. These community leaders may include politicians, ministers, the media, and charitable agencies. They also may seek support from employees they have already organized at other employers. These employees might be the ones leafleting. They might appear at a union meeting and extol the benefits they have received from being union members.

Unions also may reach into their bag of dirty tricks. Sometimes unions will station a loudspeaker truck outside the gates, blaring the union message for hours at a time. They might show up with a large inflatable rat or some other loathsome animal as a caricature of the employer or its policies.

As noted earlier, they will often try to bait supervisors into committing unfair labor practices. Sometimes union business agents will try to provoke a public debate with a company official in the presence of a group of employees. The business agent who does this for a living usually wins the debate against the company representative who may have little experience in union campaigns. Some unscrupulous union supporters resort to sabotage, false (usually anonymous) reports to authorities about illegal employer conduct, or safety complaints to OSHA (Occupational Safety and

Health Administration). The idea is to stir things up, keeping the employer off balance and on the defensive.

Although an employer cannot ignore what the union is doing and saying, the more successful employers stay on the offensive and stick to their "game plan." The employer that believes it must respond to every union claim or trick will lose the election. The employer that conducts a positive campaign has a much better chance.

The Campaign Calendar

To assist the employer in developing a plan and sticking to it, it is often useful to devise a campaign calendar. The employer faced with a union election will determine what issues must be addressed, when they will be addressed, and how. This will ensure that employer representatives stay focused on those issues that generated the union drive in the first place and that they will deal with them in an orderly fashion. Naturally, management must remain flexible because it is common for new issues to be raised during the campaign that must be addressed. Nevertheless, the calendar can usually be easily amended to accommodate these developments.

The calendar also can help those employers who believe they need to reach a crescendo just before the election. It can also help with the issue of throwing too much information at employees. A campaign calendar will help the employer space out its campaign messages and allow for sufficient "time off" between barrages. All in all, it is a good organizational tool.

Election Day

The Preelection Conference

About a half hour before the polls are to open, the Board agent will arrive at the facility to set up the voting area and to hold a preelection conference. This conference is attended by an employer representative, the union representative, and those employees who have been designated by the union and the company to be observers (the role of observers will be discussed below). This assumes, of course, that the election will be held on company premises, which is almost always the case. Note that you must allow the outside union business representative onto company premises for purposes of this preelection conference and for the counting of the ballots once the polls close. This does not mean, however, that you must allow him/her free access to all parts of the facility. The representative should be made to report his/her arrival, escorted to the preelection conference, and then escorted out until it is time to count the ballots, where a similar procedure should be followed.

The purpose of the preelection conference is to go over the details of the election procedure and instruct the observers on their duties.

Prior to the conference, the employer will provide the Board with a voter list. If someone who is not on this list tries to vote, his/her vote will be challenged by the

Board agent (more on challenges below). Each observer (who will be a nonsupervisory employee of the employer) will mark off the names of voters on the list as they vote. Observers may also challenge voters. If you believe someone will try to vote (such as a discharged employee), you should instruct your observer to challenge the individual if the Board agent does not do so.

The Mechanics of Setting Up the Polls

The voting booth is usually a portable one, which folds up for easy transportation and has canvas sides. Many people feel that the entrance to the voting booth should face away from the observers and Board agent for maximum privacy. The Board agent also will have posters designating the area as a polling place and note that electioneering is prohibited. Employers also use the preelection conference to inspect the voting booth to ensure no one has scrawled a union slogan on the inside of the booth.

Another "ritual" performed at the preelection conference is the preparation of the ballot box and inspection of the ballots. The ballot box is made of cardboard and is prepared using masking tape or something similar. The parties will ensure that there are no premarked ballots already inside the box (I've never found any in thirty years.). The ballot itself is described below.

Occasionally, union observers will be wearing hats, buttons, or other insignia promoting the union or disparaging management. You should ask the Board agent to require them to remove such gear and place it out of sight. The Board agent may or may not accede to your request (Board law has vacillated on this issue). At least, however, you have made a "record" of your objection and may use this later on to file an objection to the election if the company loses.

Once the preelection conference is completed, all personnel should leave the polling area except for the Board agent and the observers.

The Role of the Observers

As noted earlier, an observer will be a nonmanagement employee of the company. Supervisors, union business agents, and the like are not allowed to be observers. Other than these restrictions, the company and the union can pick whomever they want to fulfill this function. In most elections, there will be only one or two observers per side. From management's point of view, the company observer should be someone who is a member of the bargaining unit, who is mature, and can be trusted to perform the duties of the position.

Although the Board agent will instruct the observers at the preelection conference, you should also instruct them with the following:

- Challenge anyone not on the voter roster unless the Board agent challenges them first.
- Challenge other specific people you may designate, if any.

- Challenge anyone who appears to vote who has not provided proper identification or who you know is not an employee of the company.
- Note any unusual or disruptive activity (such as arguments between the union observer and a voter) and report the same to management immediately after the election.
- Do not hesitate to challenge a voter or to object to disruptive conduct, but do not engage in arguments with the union observer or Board agent. Simply state the challenge or objection and leave it at that.

The Voting Process

Once the room is prepared, the Board agent will wait for the time of the polls to open. Many times employees will already be lined up outside the door to the room. Employees will enter the room one at a time (except in cases involving large numbers of employees where there may be more than one voting booth), identify themselves, be handed a ballot, and enter the voting booth. The ballot itself is very simple. Basically the question on the ballot is: "Do you want to be represented by the union for purposes of collective bargaining?"

The voter will then check one of two blocks: yes or no. After voting, the employee will fold the ballot in half and deposit it in the ballot box and leave the area. Board agents are very good at voting large numbers of employees in a short period of time and, as you can see, the process is not that complicated.

Ban on Electioneering in and around the Polls

The Board has a very strict rule against electioneering in the polling area. Electioneering is basically defined as soliciting for your side, criticizing the other side, or doing or saying anything to influence voters. This also can include written materials or other things of value distributed in the polling area. In one election many years ago, the union handed out free cheese to employees as they stood in line to vote. The election (which as won by the union) was later set aside by the Board.

Because of this, you should make sure that there are no antiunion posters or other literature of this nature in the polling area. The only thing relating to the election that should appear in the voting area is the "big blue notice" sent by the Board and referred to earlier. Make sure your observer notifies you of any electioneering he/she observes.

Where Should You Be during the Voting?

The simple answer is that you, and all other members of management, should be as far away from the polling area as possible. Any appearance of management around the polling area can lead to charges of electioneering, coercion, or surveillance. This is why you must pick observers who can be trusted to monitor the situation for you.

Some supervisors have told me that their offices are right across the hall from the polling area. I tell them to leave their offices and go somewhere else. Other management personnel, even those office staff who are not involved with the bargaining unit in any way, should stay away from this area. Naturally, work must go on, but this should be a consideration in choosing the place of the polls, not an excuse for having management in and around the polling area.

The Challenge Process

We have referred to challenges and the reasons for challenges. Now we will discuss the actual procedure on how challenged votes are handled. If a voter is challenged, he/she will still vote as described above. After voting but before the ballot is placed in the box, the ballot will be placed in a sealed envelope, the employee will sign his/her name on the envelope (not the ballot itself), and the envelope will then be deposited in the ballot box. We will discuss later what is done with these challenged ballots.

Counting the Ballots

Once the polls have closed, the Board agent will give the parties a few minutes for their representatives to return to the polling area. After that, he/she will open the ballot box, empty the ballots onto a table, ensure no ballots are remaining in the box, and begin counting. Once again, both observers and company representatives should observe this process to see that each ballot is counted and counted properly as either a yes or a no. Occasionally, someone will sign his/her name on a ballot that will invalidate it. Others will write slogans or other extraneous material on the ballot. Usually, these ballots will be counted unless it is impossible to determine the intent of the voter. Once the counting is done, the first thing the Board agent must determine is if the challenged ballots could have affected the result of the election. If they do not, the process is basically over and the agent will complete the tally sheet and announce the winner. If challenges could affect the result, the Board must resolve the challenges in a later proceeding. This means the result of the election could be up in the air for a while. Sometimes, the Board agent will try to get the parties to agree on a challenge on the spot. It is usually wise not to do this without consulting with a legal advisor.

A labor election is to decide by a majority *of those who vote*. Notice that it is *not* a majority of employees in the bargaining unit. Thus, if you assume a one hundred employee unit and only forty employees vote and twenty-one vote for the union, the union wins. Employees, many of whom may be reluctant to vote for various reasons, must be told of this rule. Informing them that their votes do count may help prevent the fate of the entire bargaining unit being deciding by a minority of employees. Typically speaking, union-oriented employees are more likely to vote, so you must overcome the reluctance of others to go to the polls. If you lose the election then so be it, but all employees should have a voice.

I am often asked what happens in case of a tie vote. This does happen occasionally. The answer is that ties go the employer because a majority of employees have not voted for union representation.

Objections to the Election

If you lose the election, you must decide if there is any basis to challenge the result. Common objections are unfair labor practices, violation of laboratory standards, or unlawful electioneering. You must make this decision quickly since the Board only allows you seven (7) calendar days from the time ballots are tallied to file such objections. If objections are timely filed, the regional director will usually hold a hearing to resolve the objections. His/her decision is subject to review by the Board.

Bar Rules

Once the process described above is completed, one might ask, "How often can an employer and employees be put through such an ordeal?" The answer comes in the form of what are referred to as "bar" rules. These rules bar subsequent petitions from being filed for certain periods of time. The purpose of the bar rules are to give the parties some labor peace for a while and also to allow a union that has won an election a period of time in which to obtain a contract for the employees represented by it without having to fight off a petition by a rival union or a decertification petition (an election where employees try to kick out the union).

Election Bar

If the union loses the election, the Board will issue a document called Certificate of Results of Election. Under this scenario, no petitions by a rival union can be filed with regard to the same bargaining unit in which the previous election was conducted for a period of one year from the date of the election. This does not mean another union cannot start organizing your employees before this time has elapsed. It merely means they have to wait the one year period before filing the petition. The "bar" rules bar the filing of a petition, and nothing else.

Certification Bar

If the union wins the election, the Board will issue a document entitled Certification of Representative. This will bar a petition by a rival union or a decertification petition for one year from the date of the certification. As noted above, the purpose of the Certification Bar is twofold: (1) to give a time of labor peace and (2) to give the newly elected bargaining agent (the union) a period of time to negotiate the first labor contract with the employer.

Contract Bar

If the union succeeds in obtaining a contract, petitions by rival unions and decertification petitions will be barred for the duration of the contract with two important exceptions. First, during a thirty-day window between the ninetieth and sixtieth day prior to contract expiration, a petition may be filed. This rule is to allow for a change in bargaining agent or for employees to reject the union through an election. Otherwise, an employer and union could renew their contract before its expiration and effectively bar any petitions forever.

Second, some contracts are very lengthy, lasting for years. In order to give employees a chance to elect a new union or to decertify the incumbent union, the Board has adopted a rule that a contract bar will only bar petitions for up to three years. This is currently the length of most labor agreements anyway. Thus, a contract that lasts for five years will only serve as a bar for the first three years of the contract's life.

Naturally, once a labor contract has expired, but there is no renewal agreement in place, a petition may be filed at any time.

Types of Election Petitions

RC Petition

This is the type of petition we have been discussing at some length. It is where a union seeks to become the bargaining representative for the employees in a given bargaining unit.

RD Petition

This is a decertification petition where employees seek to remove a labor organization as their bargaining representative. The rules are very similar as those for RC petitions. For instance, the petition must be supported by at least 30 percent of employees in the unit. It must be filed with the Board and is subject to all the rules regarding eligibility of voters, Excelsior lists, and the other items discussed above. **Employers may not give any substantive assistance to employees in a decertification attempt.** Additionally, they must not encourage employees to decertify their union. If employees come to you with questions about decertification, tell them the law restricts what you can say to them at this point and refer them to the nearest Board office. It is okay to confirm to them that there does exist a decertification process and to supply them with the address and phone number of the Board. Beyond that, you should not go.

Once a decertification petition has been filed, however, the employer may engage in campaigning pursuant to the rules discussed above in sections "What Do You Do If Your Business Is Subject to a Union Organizing Drive" and "The Ins and Outs of a Labor Election."

RM Petition

This is a relatively rare petition although recent Board law has resulted in greater use. This is a petition filed by management when they have a good faith uncertainty that the union no longer represents a majority of the employees in the bargaining unit. It is sometimes filed by management when faced with recognitional picketing to speed up the time of an election. The good faith uncertainty must be supported by objective evidence of the same. This might include a signature list of employees presented to management stating that they no longer desire the union. Another example would be oral statements of a number of employees to this same effect. Long periods of inactivity by the union, i.e., the union has disappeared, has in the past supported a RM petition. Employer speculation about employee desires or statements from a few people will usually not suffice and the Board will dismiss the petition. If the Board processes the petition, however, an election will be scheduled and this will follow basically the same rules as discussed above regarding RC elections.

UD Elections

These elections are quite rare. A UD petition is one supported by at least 30 percent of the bargaining unit members. The purpose is to remove from the labor contract the union security provision that requires employees to join the union and remain members in good standing as a condition of employment. Such elections may be held no more frequently than once in every twelve-month period.

UC Petitions

These petitions do not involve an election at all and may be filed by either union or management. The purpose of such petitions is to request the Board to consider clarifying the composition of a bargaining unit. These often take place where the Board's original certification may have left open questions about whether a certain group of employees was included in the unit. These petitions also may be filed when the job status of a particular classification has changed. For instance, perhaps a job once was considered supervisory in nature and excluded from the unit. Later on, the supervisory duties were removed. These cases are decided by the Board, not a secret ballot election. UC petitions may be filed at any time and are not subject to normal contract bar rules.

One word of caution here. Unions will often try to use a UC petition as a substitute for a secret ballot election when a new group of employees are added to the workforce. The employer often opposes the UC petition and argues to the Board that the employees in the new category should have the opportunity to vote.

UA Petitions

Once again, these petitions do not involve an election or authorization cards. They may be filed by management or union. The purpose is to amend the certification originally granted by the Board. For instance if a union has merged with another union since the original certification, there may be a need to amend the certification by adding the new name of the union. A similar procedure could take place if the company was bought and subsumed into a new entity.

A Word about the Employee Free Choice Act

At the time this book went to publication, legislation was pending that, if enacted in its current form, would greatly change the rules regarding labor law in the situation where a union is trying to organize the employees and, if successful, negotiating the first labor contract.

This law would mandate employer recognition if the union had obtained signatures on authorization cards from a majority of employees in the bargaining unit. It is unclear if the employer could challenge the proposed unit or make other challenges through a representation hearing. In any event, the law substitutes a card majority for a secret ballot election in these situations. Apparently the law would not change the rules on decertification or other types of elections.

There are also major changes pertaining to the negotiation of the first contract. Basically, if the company and the union cannot agree to the provisions of a first contract within six months, they must submit the outstanding disputed provisions to binding arbitration.

The law also would impact awards of back pay. The damages available to an employee fired during an organizing campaign are increased from back pay to triple back pay.

Finally, an employer is subject for a fine of up to $20,000 per violation if it is found guilty of unfair labor practices committed during the organizing campaign or during the bargaining for a new contract. Currently, there is no such provision in the law.

No one knows if the Employee Free Choice Act will ever become law or, if so, what its ultimate provisions will be. You are advised to check with your legal advisors or trade publications on the status of this proposed legislation.

Chapter 4

Living with a Union

Introduction

Having a union at your facility is certainly not tantamount to the end of the world. Many companies have had a unionized workforce for many years. In a lot of these cases, the relations between company and the union are businesslike and often mutually beneficial. On the other hand, some relationships are characterized by mistrust, rancor, and constant bickering. Which one of these relationships you have may be largely out of your control. Although it is possible to repair a damaged relationship, it is difficult and takes a long time.

My experience is that **most relationships sour because of a lack of trust**. It has often occurred to me that the company–union relationship is more akin to an unhappy marriage (in many ways) than it is to a normal business relationship. That is, the parties are often stuck with each other for better or for worse. If a company you do business with overcharges or cheats you, you merely cease doing business and go to someone else. Not so in a union relationship. You may feel that the union has taken advantage of you. The union may feel that you have taken advantage of it. The problem is you can't just walk away. You must work through your problems in an honest and forthright way. You should never lie or mislead. This is not to say you have to bare your soul and give away company secrets or strategy. If the union asks a question you do not want to answer, tell the union it's none of its business (or maybe something gentler) rather than make up something.

Unions do not expect the company to agree with them all the time. Unions do not expect the company to do things that are detrimental to it just to please the union. Unions do not expect the company to "give away the candy store"; in fact, unions do not want that. A viable, profitable company is just as much in the interest of the union as it is the company. The union just wants a bit more of the profit to go to employees in the form of wages and benefits than you might otherwise want to give. This allows the union to receive dues from grateful employees who, in turn, keep the union in business itself and pays the salaries of union officials. There is nothing wrong with this. This is just the way things work.

What most unions do expect, however, is an open and honest relationship and for their officers and stewards to be treated with civility. The company should insist on the same from the union. To be sure, there are unions (or locals of unions) out there that subscribe to a "gotcha" theory of labor relations and will try to get away with everything they can even if they have to lie, cheat, or steal to get it. Hopefully, you will not encounter such a situation. If you do, you must maintain your integrity, but be watchful at all times. Sometimes, the international body of the union will intervene to "reel in" a rogue local. In any event, it is plain to see how damaging such a situation can be when the parties are trying to get along from day to day and live under the provisions of the labor agreement.

Bargaining for a Contract

The Duty to Bargain in Good Faith

We have already discussed, in Chapter 3, Section 8(d) of the National Labor Relations Act, which defines the duty to bargain in good faith. In the context of contract negotiations, this means a willingness to meet at reasonable times to negotiate a labor agreement. It also means having a sincere desire to reach agreement if terms acceptable to you can be reached. It means an obligation to put any agreement that is reached into a written form and to sign it.

As discussed earlier, the duty to bargain in good faith does not mean, however, that you have to make concessions or agree to things that you do not believe are in your best interests. It does not mean you must agree on a labor contract at all.

One wonders then, why management and labor usually do reach agreement. The answer is that because management and labor are in a sense joined at the hip, it is in the best interest of both to come to an agreement because the absence of an agreement spells uncertainty. It invites strikes and lockouts. It can distract both management and employees from their duties. Having a contract means a period of labor peace will follow. Everyone knows what the rules are under a contract and that the contract will be in force for several years.

Sometimes I am asked if management is obliged to talk about certain topics during collective bargaining. Usually my answer is "yes." Over the years, the law has determined that almost any subject that could affect wages, benefits, or other terms and conditions of employment is a *mandatory* subject of bargaining. That is, you must talk about it at the table until you come to agreement or impasse (a concept that will be explained later).

There are a few subjects of bargaining that are known as *permissive* subjects of bargaining. They are things that the parties can talk about if they mutually agree to do so. If the parties agree to a term of the contract that is otherwise characterized as a permissible subject of bargaining, it is legally enforceable. On the other hand, a party may choose to quit talking about a permissible subject at any time. Further, you cannot insist that the other side agree to your proposal on a permissible subject of bargaining to the point where it causes an impasse in the overall negotiations. Examples of permissible subjects of bargaining include collective bargaining provisions covering supervisors, provisions regarding the marketing of the employers' product or the pricing of it, indemnification bonds, and internal union organization and operations.

There is a third category of bargaining subjects known as *illegal* subjects of bargaining. As the name implies, the parties are prohibited from talking about illegal subjects of bargaining, even if both want to negotiate in this area. Any agreement on an illegal subject of bargaining will be unenforceable and likely result in an unfair labor practice charge or a lawsuit. Some examples include: clauses that require discrimination on the basis of race, sex, national origin, age, religion, disability, or other grounds prohibited by law; "hot cargo" agreements whereby the employer agrees not to handle the goods of employers who do not have contracts with the union; closed shop provisions that require employees to be union members before they are ever hired; and hiring hall agreements that give preference to union members.

The Duty to Exchange Information

Prior to or even during contract negotiations, the union may ask for certain information from the company to assist it in discharging its bargaining duty. Such information could consist of current wage rates, a seniority roster, the cost of health insurance and premiums paid by employees, and other data. Your initial reaction might be to refuse to provide this information because it is confidential. In the labor law context, however, you would have committed a breach of the duty to bargain in good faith, a Section 8(a)(5) violation. The law has long been that a union is entitled to obtain information from the company that is relevant to its role as bargaining agent. Theoretically, the employer has an equal right to request information of the union. Most employers, however, do not do this because the union will have very little information to provide.

Sometimes, claims will be made at the bargaining table by one party (usually the employer) that give the other party the right to request information backing up the assertion. The classic example is the employer who says it cannot afford to pay the union's wage or benefit demands. This will give the union the right to review the financial records of the employer to see if its "claim of poverty" is supportable. The employer may be able to attach conditions to this review (such as, it must be performed by a professional accountant, any documents reviewed must remain confidential, etc.), but the employer will have to give the union access. A tip: If what you mean to say is that your think the union's demand is too high, ridiculous, or not supported by the market, say that. Don't say you can't afford to pay, unless that is really the case. Sometimes during bargaining, unions will make a claim that allows the employer to make an information request. For instance, if the union claims that all local industry contracts it has with employers require a certain level of wages or certain benefits, the employer may ask the union to furnish it with copies of said contracts so the employer can verify the union's claim.

The duty to exchange information also arises in the course of grievance administration and arbitration, but this aspect of the duty will be discussed below.

Preparing for Contract Negotiations

Like all other events that are important and complicated, you must prepare for contract negotiations in order to succeed. Even though you may not be at the negotiating table, you may still be asked to help those who will be getting ready for the contract talks.

Who Is Involved?

Preparation for labor contract negotiations should involve representatives from various parts of the company. Usually these would include operations, finance and accounting, executive management, human resources/benefits, marketing, and vendor/customer relations. Each will have a contribution to make even though people from these groups may not always come to the bargaining table.

Set and Prioritize Goals

It is good to set bargaining goals just as you would in any other business plan. These might include to pay no more than a certain percentage of wage/benefit increases, to make a particular clause of the contract more favorable, to remove a provision of the contract that has caused trouble, etc. Once goals are set they should be prioritized. As a part of this goal setting, management should explore concessions it may be willing to give in order to obtain these goals. After all, bargaining is a two-way street.

Some companies formulate an initial proposal and present it at the first bargaining session. Others prefer to wait until they receive the union proposal and then submit theirs later.

Strike Preparation

One important part of preparation is to prepare for a strike. Fortunately, strikes usually do not happen, but it's always a possibility. It is crucial that management be ready to deal with a strike. For example:

- The decision should be made ahead of time whether the company will operate during a strike and, if so, whether it will hire replacement workers or try to run the facility with supervisory or other nonbargaining unit personnel.
- The company should designate those who will be responsible for dealing with the media, customers, and vendors, and how and when these companies will be informed of a strike.
- Some companies prepare notices to the local unemployment compensation office informing the office that the employees on an attached list are on strike. Strikers do not receive unemployment compensation benefits in most states.
- Security measures should be examined and strengthened if necessary.
- Sometimes supervisors and other non-union employees, who may be called upon to perform bargaining unit jobs, are given training on how to perform these functions.
- The company should check with its insurance carriers to determine how long employees will remain covered if the company stops paying its share of premiums and understand whether COBRA notices will be required and who will be responsible for this.
- Ensure that the company knows where the exact physical boundaries of its facility are so that it can determine if strikers are trespassing.
- If the company leases the facility, notify the owner at some point of the possibility of a strike and enlist his/her support.

Information Gathering

Another important part of preparation for contract negotiation is to assemble information that may be useful during bargaining. This might include demographic information on the employees, such as age, seniority, amount of sick days taken in the past, average vacation entitlement, median and mean wage, and hours worked including overtime. It also should include cost of health insurance and other similar benefits and estimates of how much these costs will increase. Employee usage of health insurance benefits might be informative as well, including how many spent over their deductible amounts. Any anticipated changes in the tax codes that could increase labor costs also must be a part of this information-gathering process.

It is advisable to gather comparative information as well, such as what similar businesses in the local community are paying or what other companies in the same industry are paying. The same holds true for benefits, such as health insurance, vacations, etc. Ideally, you should obtain a recent wage and benefit survey from a local Chamber of Commerce, trade organization, or private survey agency. In many instances, your company must participate in such a survey before you will be entitled to see the results. It is well worth providing the information, in my opinion. Particular attention should be paid to trends in local union contracts in similar businesses. Sometimes this information is hard to get if it is not contained in the surveys mentioned above. Perhaps, however, a contact in another company would be willing to provide the information if you would be prepared to reciprocate.

The Negotiation Team

Once the above preparations are made, the company must decide who will be at the bargaining table and who the chief spokesperson will be. There is no "typical" in this as companies are different. What I have seen mostly, however, is that the company's team is composed of a high ranking executive (rarely the CEO or top official, however), someone from human resources, and one or two people from operations. Other specialists, such as finance officers or benefits experts, may be brought into negotiations when their particular subject will be discussed at the table.

Whoever is at the table, one of them should be designated as the official note-taker for the company. This should not be the chief spokesperson because he or she needs to be either talking or listening to the other side and should not be distracted by having to take official notes. These notes should be typed shortly after each session has ended and reviewed by the other members of the team for accuracy. There is no need to show these notes to the union. The notes can come in handy if there is some difference in opinion over what was said at the table or if memories need to be refreshed. The notes also may be useful if a refusal to bargain unfair labor practice charge is filed. Indeed, the NLRB can subpoena your notes and those of the union. I am sometimes asked if bargaining sessions can be recorded, either electronically or by a court reporter or stenographer. My answer is that this is one of those permissive subjects of bargaining and, therefore, it is only if the union and company agree that such recording can take place. My recommendation is against recording. The parties need to be free to voice frank opinions, sometime in not so gentle terms. Having a tape recorder or stenographer there will inhibit this exchange of views and do a disservice to all concerned. The notes taken by the note taker need not be verbatim, but they should be accurate and fairly describe what took place.

The First Session

Usually, the first negotiation session will be limited to introductions, exchange of assurances of goodwill, etc., and the exchange of initial proposals (as noted earlier, sometimes only the union will have an initial proposal at this first session). The ground rules for the negotiations are usually set forth at the first session. Typical of such rules is an agreement that the parties will bargain about noneconomic matters first and thereafter bargain about economics. Another standard agreement is that all agreements reached on individual articles or provisions of the contract are tentative until overall agreement is reached. It also is useful to agree that when agreement is reached on a particular article, it will be reduced to written form and initialed by both sides.

The Typical Process

After the first meeting, a typical scenario is that the parties will begin to negotiate on the various noneconomic articles of the contract; those provisions without a direct economic cost, such as management rights, seniority, recognition, and work rules. Many negotiators think it is best to start out with these clauses, which will be the least controversial. This creates a precedent of agreement and builds some momentum that will hopefully carry over when the more contentious provisions are addressed.

Once the noneconomic provisions are either agreed to or tabled, the parties will address the economic parts of the contract: wages, benefits, vacation, premium pay for overtime, call out and shift work, etc.

During the negotiations, the chief negotiators for each side will often have "side bar" or private conferences. I have found these to be useful in many situations. So many times, the spokespersons feel the need to posture a bit while they are at the table in front of their constituents. Sidebar meetings often serve an important purpose when the negotiators can communicate in a more frank and open manner. It is important that if your counterpart tells you something in confidence in such a meeting, that you respect this and expect the same of him or her.

Some Pointers

Although the art of negotiation is beyond the scope of this book, there are a few thoughts worth sharing:

- Do not lie to the other side; if you don't want to reveal something say so.
- Try to get a concession for every concession you make, not necessarily at the same time.
- Save your important concessions for last.
- Do not make a concession too readily; call a caucus (a private meeting of your side of the table and discuss it).
- Don't allow yourself to be rushed by the union; once again, if you want to call a caucus or call it quits for the day, then do so.
- Don't be forced into meeting late into the night or on weekends. There is no requirement that you do so if you don't want to. We all need our rest and we need to get away from the table for reasonable periods of time to assess what has happened and plan for future sessions.

- Don't engage in name calling. Notice that I am not saying you should refrain from strong language, just don't refer to the other person in an offensive manner.
- Don't belittle or intentionally embarrass your opposite number in front of his/her negotiation team members. If you feel a need to do this, do it in private.
- Don't give undue attention to proposals that you know will never be acceptable.
- Subject to the point immediately above, don't be reluctant to have the other side explain its proposals and ask them how they would work in given situations; this process often uncovers deficiencies in the proposal and may result in its withdrawal or amendment.
- When you make a proposal, do it in a way that projects an expectation that it will be accepted. In other words, don't apologize for your proposal or preface it with a statement such as, "You are not going to like this but ..." Explain the purpose of your proposal and how it will work without being asked to do so. Answer any questions honestly and as objectively as possible.
- If you become convinced a proposal you have made is unworkable, withdraw it.
- Don't ever refuse to talk about a mandatory subject of bargaining until you believe impasse has been reached; it's better to talk about a subject more than necessary rather than less.
- Keep an open mind. Be prepared to change your opinion or game plan if confronted with evidence that you should do so. Demand the same of the other side.
- Learn how to say "no" in several ways. Sometimes you want to (metaphorically) slam the door, other times you want to leave the door slightly ajar, other times you may want to leave the door open wide but are not yet ready to accede to the proposal.
- Listen to what the other side is saying. If you do not understand, have them explain. Expect them to do the same with you.
- Do everything you can to get the commitment from each member of the union team that he/she will recommend to the members that they ratify any agreement to which the negotiators agree.

Ratification

All union constitutions that I have read require that the employer's final contract proposal be presented to the members for ratification, usually by a simple majority of those who vote. Even though the bargaining teams may have agreed to a contract, the contract is not effective or legally binding until the members have ratified it. Naturally, the employer is not invited to such meetings to plead its case. This is why it is so important that the union bargaining team members recommend ratification to the members.

Some employers choose to communicate with employees before the ratification vote by mail or other mass communication. This is permissible so long as you do not appear to be negotiating directly with the members, which is prohibited by law. You must limit any such communication to a summary of what has been agreed to and why you took the positions you did and the advantages of the proposed contract. You also may encourage the members to ratify the contract. Whether you do this or not depends on a host of factors. Usually, the most important factor is whether the union bargaining committee will recommend ratification. If they have indicated they will not, or if the recommendation will not be unanimous, you should seriously consider directly communicating with the membership.

On the other hand, if the committee is going to unanimously recommend ratification, they may view it as an insult that you are communicating with the members recommending the same thing. In other words, they may view it as interference.

If the members do not ratify the contract, then the result is usually further bargaining. How long this goes on depends on the situation. This always puts the employer in a bad situation because, if it sweetens the pie as the result of a failure to ratify, some members will get the impression that rejection of the contract proposal will lead to more for them. This establishes a dangerous precedent. Some employers in this situation are willing to move money from one area of the contract to another, but not to increase the overall offer.

If the contract is ratified, then it is signed by appropriate officials of both the company and the union and becomes effective. Some unions require a representative of the international body to approve the contract.

The Bermuda Rectangle of Labor Law: The Relationship and Interaction of Contract Expiration Date–Impasse–the Duty to Bargain–and the Right to Strike

We could have characterized this as the Bermuda Pentagon if we were to include the right to lockout, but four concepts at a time are enough for anyone. We will deal with lockouts later (they don't happen that often, anyway).

Although the above concepts do interact in strange ways sometimes, the basic rules are easy to understand. It is, however, crucial to understand them because this is one of the key areas of labor law and one that is most confusing to those who have not approached the study of these ideas in a logical manner. Hopefully, the discussion in this book will provide that "logical manner" for you.

Here are the rules:

- The union cannot strike until the contract has expired (assuming the contract contains a no-strike clause—all contracts I have seen contain such a clause).
- The parties must continue to bargain until they have reached an impasse.
- Contract expiration does not constitute an impasse.

■ A strike does not constitute an impasse and, therefore, you must continue to bargain with the union even though it is on strike until impasse is reached.

■ If impasse is reached before contract expiration, the old contract must still be observed.

■ If the old contract expires and the parties are still bargaining (i.e., impasse has not been reached), the employer must keep the terms and conditions of the old contract in effect until impasse or until a new contract is reached.

■ Once impasse is reached, the employer may (but is not required to) implement the terms of its final offer, assuming the old contract has expired (or once the old contract has expired). The employer cannot implement any term that was not fairly encompassed in its final offer. In other words, if you offered a 5 percent wage increase in your final offer, you cannot implement a 4 percent increase or vice versa. On many occasions, employers will implement only the economic terms of the final offer, leaving the old contract in place for all other terms, such as seniority, discipline and discharge, etc.

■ Once impasse has been reached, the duty to bargain is suspended unless the impasse is later broken. This is why the employer may implement its final offer upon impasse (assuming the old contract has expired).

■ An impasse is broken by any substantial change in circumstances that make it likely that further bargaining may be successful. For instance, the willingness of one party to change its position on an item that contributed to the impasse. A strike has often been held to break an impasse, oddly enough.

■ An employer that has implemented its final proposal after impasse is not obliged to "unimplement" the proposal after an impasse has been broken and the parties have resumed bargaining. The implemented proposal may remain in place until a new agreement is reached or until another impasse is reached.

Contract Extension Agreements

Sometimes the parties are bargaining, but will be unable to conclude a deal before the old contract expires. In these cases, the parties often enter into a contract extension agreement. Such agreements are advantageous to employers because, if the contract is extended, the no-strike clause remains effective. Also, the no lockout clause remains in effect, so the employer cannot lock out employees. Usually, contract extension agreements have a certain date for expiration. Sometimes they allow a party to give a certain amount of notice (seventy-two hours, for example) that they desire to terminate the extension agreement.

Contract extension agreements are useful tools to keep negotiations going within the framework of the existing contract. They should not, however, be used as a crutch for less than efficient negotiations. Unions often demand that any wage increase be retroactive to contract expiration, thus the delay caused by such agreements in reaching a final deal can come with a price. Also, such agreements take the pressure off of both sides. You may not want this. You may want to pressure the union to accept your offer. The opposite situation may be the case as well. Whether you enter into such an agreement should be carefully weighed.

Strike Notification Agreements

This is an agreement that is sometimes used when the parties are bargaining, but the old contract has expired, or is about to expire. Such agreements require the union to give the company a certain amount of notice (e.g., forty-eight hours) before they strike. The utility of such agreements is obvious. Rather than the union being able to strike with no notice and catch the company unaware, the company would have some minimal time to prepare. Unions are under no compulsion to enter into such agreements.

The Role of Union Stewards, Business Agents, Etc.

The union is a hierarchy just like most other business organizations. At the top of the hierarchy is the international union with its top officers and staff. Then there are the regional divisions with their top officers and staff.

It is usually rare for an employer representative to deal with any of the above individuals. The union officials you usually will deal with will be the union employee who is in charge of servicing the local (they are called by different names, but, for purposes of this book, we will refer to them as business agent), local union officers, and the union steward.

The business agent is a paid union employee. He/she may service only the employees of your bargaining unit, but it is more likely that he/she will have obligations to other bargaining units located at numerous, individual companies throughout a city or other geographical area. My experience is that these people are sometimes "stretched thin." This may make it difficult to reach them or they may seem unresponsive. Be persistent and document your attempts to contact them. Nevertheless, try to understand that they may have responsibilities that extend beyond your workplace.

You will most likely encounter the business agent in four situations: contract negotiation, step two or higher of the grievance process, discussion of serious problems that affect the unit as a whole (e.g., upcoming layoffs), and labor arbitrations. Although the business agent is not an employee of the company, he/she often has a right under the contract to reasonable access to employees to discuss union business. Naturally, such access should not interfere with the work of the employees or disrupt the business in any way. Additionally, he/she does not have carte blanche to roam the facility at will. You can designate a space for any discussions. Many labor contracts specify in detail what rights the business agent has in this regard.

Most companies and unions have developed protocols (often unwritten) on when the company should contact the business agent and when contacting a steward is appropriate. Generally speaking, the business agent should be contacted for any out of the ordinary issue, whereas the steward can be contacted for routine discipline and day-to-day items. While this may not be a very descriptive dichotomy, it is really the best we can do because the relationships between company officials and union officials are so different from business-to-business and from union-to-union.

The union stewards are at the bottom of the union hierarchy. This, however, does not mean they are unimportant; quite the contrary. The steward functions as the "eyes and ears" of the union inside the workplace. In many cases, the steward is the only representative of the union that most employees see on a routine bases. He/she often "is the union" to many of your workers. Stewards usually handle day-to-day complaints and questions raised by employees. Usually these matters pertain to alleged unfair treatment or violations of the labor contract. The steward's role is to approach his/her contact person within the company (a supervisor, plant foreman, industrial relations official) and try to resolve the problem without filing a grievance or bringing in the business agent.

To their credit, most such problems are resolved "locally" in this manner. They are not always resolved in favor of the union. Sometimes there is a misunderstanding or the steward is convinced by the company that the union is misreading the contract or that alleged facts upon which a complaint is based are not as they appeared. On the other hand, sometimes the steward points out a practice or problem that does violate the contract and of which responsible company officials were unaware. In any event, this clearing of the air is good for both union and management and should be encouraged.

How many stewards are present at any given facility depends on the size of the workforce, whether there are multiple shifts, and a host of other factors. Sometime the labor agreement contains provisions limiting the number of stewards, specifying their rights, and other matters. It is usually common for the contract to require that the union notify the company in writing who their stewards will be and if there are any changes.

Stewards must be given a reasonable amount of time to investigate complaints and otherwise carry out their duties. There is no requirement that they be paid for this time and, like the business agent, they are not allowed to disrupt the operations of the facility. Some agreements require that stewards be paid for at least some of the time they spend investigating grievances.

Any disciplinary action taken against a steward should be undertaken very carefully. There is always a possibility that the union will claim you are taking action against stewards due to their activities on behalf of the union. This would be unlawful discrimination in violation of Section 8(a)(3) of the Act. Stewards have a certain amount of leeway in arguing the union's case to the employer in the context of complaints, grievances, and the like. Strong language that would not be tolerated from a rank and file employee on the shop floor must sometimes be overlooked if it comes from a steward advocating for the union's cause. There are limits on this and most stewards conduct themselves professionally. Nevertheless, if you are considering taking action against a steward because of his/her conduct in the course of performing steward duties, it is best to seek legal advice first.

Steward may either be elected by the membership or appointed by the union, depending on the labor organization involved. Sometimes the steward position is a stepping stone to a full-time position on the union's payroll as a business agent or other type of union representative.

Officers of the local union usually include a president, vice president(s), secretary, treasurer, and others. They are elected by the membership. Sometimes these individual are just figure heads and sometimes they have real power, especially the president of the local. On occasion, the president of the local will have a role in contract negotiations or in grievance handling. This depends on the union's by-laws and, sometimes, on the personalities involved.

One important thing to remember: You do not get to pick with whom you deal. The law requires you to deal with the union's chosen representative, just as the union must deal with whomever the company designates as its representative. This is not to say that you can't complain to the union representative's boss, but such pleas often fall of deaf ears.

The local union also will have various committees in place. These are usually composed of a handful of employees from the bargaining unit. They may contain some stewards, but this is not always the case. Sometimes they are chaired by a local officer. The most common committees with which management will deal will be the bargaining committee and the grievance committee. The bargaining committee helps formulate contract demands based on member input. Most of its members will usually be at the negotiating table.

The grievance committee screens grievances for merit or lack of merit and recommends to the business agent whether grievances should go forward. Members of this committee will often be present during grievance meetings and may assist if the case goes to arbitration.

As with the union steward, you should be careful before disciplining any member of a union committee, especially if the discipline arises from their performance of union functions.

Chapter 5

Introduction to a Collective Bargaining Agreement

Terminology

A collective bargaining agreement is a contract between a labor organization (union) and a company setting forth terms and conditions of employment for the employees in the bargaining unit. It is sometimes referred to as a labor contract, labor agreement, union contract, or other terms; all mean the same thing.

Some labor agreements are lengthy and some are not. Some are written in legalese and some are more plainly worded. Some have attached to them numerous letters of understanding or appendices. Some are unwieldy and some are easy to use. One common denominator is that they are all legally enforceable.

Legal Status of Collective Bargaining Agreements

A labor contract is a binding document. It is enforced most usually through the labor arbitration process when the union claims the company has violated or misapplied a term of the agreement. We will discuss arbitration in more detail later.

There is another mechanism to enforce a labor agreement. This is a lawsuit filed under Section 301 of the Labor Management Relations Act (LMRA). Often referred to as a "301 suit," this mechanism is akin to a breach of contract action. Usually, this kind of suit is filed when one party to the agreement either repudiates it or otherwise believes it is no longer obligated to abide by its terms. Depending on the precise issue involved, many courts require the complaining party to first exhaust its remedies under the arbitration clause of the agreement or else show why it would be futile to attempt resolution by arbitration.

There also may be agreements between labor and management that are not a part of the collective bargaining agreement. These may include side letters, stand alone agreements dealing with a specific issue, strike notification agreements, and the like. These agreements are enforceable as well under section 301. Whether a dispute arising under one of these separate agreements is covered under the arbitration provision of the collective bargaining will depend on the language of the arbitration clause. Also, there may be a dispute as to whether these side agreements are intended by the parties to be a part of the collective bargaining agreement.

An employer is extremely limited in what changes it can make to terms and conditions of employment during the term of the contract. Such unilateral changes often result in unfair labor practice charges for refusal to bargain with the union about such changes. Sometimes contracts give management the right to make changes, but this must be spelled out in the agreement itself. Other times, an item will be covered under management rights that usually means management has broader discretion to implement changes. Other than this, and unless there is a very good zipper clause in place (see below), unions have the right to bargain over matters that come up and that are not covered in the contract.

An important thing to understand is that, unlike in some other countries, U.S. labor law does not require collective bargaining agreements to contain certain clauses and, moreover, it does not require clauses to be worded in any specific way. For instance, parties can define seniority or deal with layoffs in any manner they choose. The law does not even require you to have a seniority clause in the agreement, although most agreements do contain such provisions. Naturally, the law does tell labor and management that there are a few clauses they cannot have in the agreement, such as a clause requiring racial discrimination or a hot cargo clause. Other than this, however, the parties are free to fashion their own agreement. The role of the law is to enforce the agreement the parties have made. With this in mind, let us review some provisions that are prevalent in labor contracts.

An Examination of Common Clauses of Collective Bargaining Agreements

Recognition Clauses

These clauses are often found near the front of the agreement. They recite that the management of the company recognizes the union as the exclusive bargaining agent for all employees in a certain unit or job category. Sometimes these clauses will cite the number of the National Labor Relations Board (NLRB) case wherein the union was certified as the bargaining agent.

Scope of Agreement Clauses

These are sometimes combined with the recognition clause. They often specify the geographical scope of the agreement, such as "the employer's facility located at 212 Main Street in Syracuse, New York" or "all the employer's facilities located within Pima County, Arizona." Some agreements go on to specifically exclude any facility or area not included in the definition. Others include what is called "after acquired clauses." These are designed to deal with the situation that arises if the employer acquires or builds another facility of a similar nature. Many such clauses require the employer to recognize the union as the agent for employees in these new locations. The legality of such clauses has been questioned because they effectively deprive the employees at the new facility of the right to vote whether or not they want a union.

Union Security Clauses

There are several possibilities as described below.

Union Shop Clause

This clause requires employees to join the union within a specified time after employment (this usually coincides with the probationary period) and to maintain such membership in good standing.

Agency Shop Clause

This clause requires employees to pay a fee to the union for its representational services, but does not require them to join the union. The service fee is equivalent to regular dues and standard assessments.

Closed Shop Clause

This clause is illegal. It requires an employee to be a member of the union before even being hired.

I have always viewed the union shop and agency shop as very similar. This is because the only thing the employee is required to do under either clause is to pay regular dues and assessments. Neither mandates that an employee go to union meetings or participate in union affairs.

Under either union or agency shop, the union may require the employer to fire the employee who has not paid regular dues and assessments. This power does not extend, however, to employees who have been expelled from the union for reasons other than nonpayment of dues, such as for antiunion behavior or conduct unbecoming a union member. Similarly, if the union fines an employee under its by-laws and the member refuses to pay, the union cannot require the employer to fire that individual.

The Checkoff Clause

This clause allows the employer to automatically deduct union dues from the employee's paycheck on a periodic basis. The employee must sign a written authorization to this effect. Such authorizations are irrevocable for a period of up to one year. Unions like the checkoff clause because they do not have to collect dues; the employer does it for them.

Please remember that, in a "right to work" state, union shops and agency shops are illegal. In other words, an employee may enjoy the benefits of union representation without having to pay dues. These people are derisively referred to as "free riders." Checkoff clauses, however, are lawful in "right to work" states. Thus, an employee who signs a checkoff authorization may be stuck with it for a year. To determine when and under what circumstances the employee may revoke the authorization, just look at the fine print on the back of the authorization document. If the employee fails to revoke the authorization at the appropriate time, most of them automatically renew for another year.

Management Rights Clause

A sample of such a clause may be found at Appendix 3. This is an important provision, at least from the viewpoint of management. This clause specifies what basic rights management possesses and does not surrender by virtue of entering into the labor agreement.

There are two approaches to such provisions. In the first approach, the clause simply says that management has all the rights it did prior to the union becoming the bargaining agent of its employees unless such rights are specifically limited by the agreement itself. In the second approach, the clause contains a "laundry list" of rights management retains (e.g., direct the work, determine the products to be produced, discharge and discipline for just cause, layoff for lack of work, determine schedules, close the business, etc.). Then, at the end of such a list, there is usually a "catch all" sentence to the effect that the list is not intended to be all inclusive. I prefer a combination of the two approaches, but either type clause, if properly drafted, should be satisfactory. Usually such clauses are found near the beginning of the agreement along with the recognition and scope of agreement clause.

No Strike—No Lockout Clause

This is another important provision for the parties. In fact, it is central to the concept of a contract that provides labor peace for the duration of its term. As its name implies, the clause specifies that the union will not strike for the duration of the contract and that management will not lock out its employees during the term of the agreement. You should be aware of a couple of nuances.

First, under current law, a sympathy strike is not banned by a no strike provision unless the term *sympathy strike* is specifically mentioned. This is where your employees cease work in sympathy for the on strike employees at another company. A common example would be where your employees make deliveries to other companies and the employees of one of these companies are on strike and have set up a picket line outside the facility. Your employees naturally do not want to cross this picket line set up by union members, even if it is a different union. Your employees refusal to make their deliveries is tantamount to a withholding of work, i.e., a strike. Unless, however, your contract specifically banned sympathy strikes, there would be little you could do to discipline your employees. Your only recourse would be to have nonbargaining unit employees make the deliveries. Sympathy strikes can arise in other contexts, but you need to be aware of this hidden danger when drafting a no strike clause. Some clauses that ban sympathy strikes contain an exception if the strike is by members of the same local union, but at a different employer.

Second, under some circumstances, employees may be permitted to strike because of safety reasons, even if a no strike clause is in existence. Section 502 of the Act (29 USC Section 143) provides, among other things that: "nor shall the quitting of labor by an employee or employees in good faith because of abnormally dangerous conditions for work at the place of employment of such employee or employees be deemed a strike under this chapter."

To fall under this exception, it must be demonstrated that the employees believed in good faith that their working conditions were abnormally dangerous; that such belief was a contributing cause to the work stoppage; that the belief was founded on ascertainable, objective evidence; and that the perceived danger posed an immediate threat of harm to the health or safety of employees.* Employees striking on this basis may not be permanently replaced, as contrasted with economic strikers.

Another provision commonly found in no strike clauses is one that specifies actions the union will take if its members strike without authorization. This is often referred to as a "wildcat strike." For instance, the provision may require the union to send a letter to its members within a specified period of time informing them that the strike is unauthorized and that they should return to work immediately. If the union complies with these requirements, the clause usually provides that the union will be relieved of any legal liability for damages caused by the wildcat strike.

---

* TNS, Inc., 309 NLRB 1348 (1992).

No strike clauses will usually specify what happens to employees who participate in an unauthorized strike. Most commonly, this means the employees will be discharged. Most contracts allow such employees, however, to make at least limited use of the grievance procedure to challenge their discharge.

Most no strike clauses contain a "laundry list" of actions—in addition to a strike—that are considered to violate the provision. This often includes slow down, sick out, work stoppage, sit-down strikes, etc. A sample no strike/no lockout clause is to be found in Appendix 4.

Grievance and Arbitration Provisions

This clause is very important from the union's viewpoint. In fact, an arbitration provision is often referred to as the *quid pro quo* (or tradeoff) for the no strike clause. The concept here is that the union is giving up its main economic weapon so it must have a way to resolve disputes that arise during the contract term. The grievance process that ends in binding arbitration by a neutral party serves this purpose very well. In fact, the U.S. Supreme Court on a number of occasions has noted the strong public policy in favor of labor arbitration. We will discuss the particulars of the grievance process and labor arbitration in more detail later on in this book.

Seniority

This is a key feature of most labor agreements. Distilled to its essence, it means that the longer you have worked at a facility, the more rights and job protection you have. Naturally, this concept stirs some controversy because merit usually has limited impact in most seniority systems. Nevertheless, seniority provisions are just as common in labor agreements as any of the clauses we have already discussed.

From a union's point of view, seniority takes away the bosses' ability to play favorites by rewarding people they like and punishing people who they do not like. Unfortunately, management often operates in this manner (or they are perceived to do so); therefore, they often have themselves to blame when employees turn to a union to eliminate such arbitrariness.

Although the central concept of seniority is easy to understand, its application in a given situation can be complicated and, at times, unwieldy and inefficient.

For instance, there are often two types of seniority provided for in the contract: usually plant seniority and departmental seniority. Plant seniority refers to length of time at the facility. Departmental seniority refers to the length of time spent within a given department. Plant seniority usually governs in cases of layoff and recall. It also is used in benefit calculations, such as pension or vacation entitlement. Departmental seniority is sometimes used for promotions within a department.

Added to this is the concept of bumping in the case of a layoff. If the employer determines to reduce the workforce, it will usually determine which departments or job classifications will be impacted. Employees who are laid off then may "bump" a less senior employee in another department or classification. This less senior employee may then use his/her seniority to bump someone else who has less seniority and so on. As you can imagine, it may take several days for the dust to clear as various employees are usually given a certain amount of time to elect to bump or be laid off.

Naturally, the employee who bumps another person must be qualified to do that person's job. Unfortunately for management, the concept of "qualification" as applied in seniority provisions is often ill defined or broadly defined.

Indeed, this arises not just in the layoff scenario, but in the case of promotions, transfers, or filling vacancies. Generally speaking the most senior employee who bids on a job gets it. However, contracts usually specify that he/she must be qualified to do the job. What does this mean? It usually does *not* mean that he/she must be the **best** qualified of those who bid. It usually does mean that the person meets *minimal* qualifications to do the work. A few contracts even award the job to the senior person even if he/she is not presently qualified to perform the duties of the position so long as he/she can become qualified within a period of time, usually thirty to ninety days.

To make things even more complex, many contracts allow the promoted employee a chance to determine if he/she likes the new job. Once again, this period may be as long as thirty days. If the employee decides he/she does not want the job, he/she may go back to his/her old position, displacing anyone who has filled in the meantime. Similarly, most contracts provide for a probationary period for the employee who was awarded a job. If, however, the company determines that the employee cannot do the job, he/she is not fired (as a probationary employee just entering the workforce would be), but rather returned to the old position.

Most contracts deal with the situation of how seniority is broken. For instance, if an employee leaves the company and comes back, does his/her seniority start over again? The answer is that it is whatever the parties can agree to in the contract. The same goes for an employee who transfers to a position outside the bargaining unit and then comes back. Most such provisions also deal with a situation of where an employee has been gone due to layoff, medical leave, work related injury, or the like. Most of these provisions allow an employee to be gone for one or two years before his/her seniority (and, therefore, his/her employment) is lost. Being discharged for just cause is also a "seniority ender." Another common provision provides that an employee's seniority is lost if he/she abandons employment or does not come to work or call in to report his/her absence for three consecutive work days.

Job bidding procedures are usually found within the seniority article. These procedures will specify how vacancies will be announced, how long employees have to bid on the position, and how long the employer has to award the job once bidding has closed. These clauses often specify how often an employee can bid on a job during a twelve-month period (to minimize disruption of the workforce caused by employees changing jobs frequently). The contract also may provide that an employee who is awarded a job but refuses it is disqualified from bidding on another job for a specified period of time. A few contracts also prohibit an employee from bidding if he/she is on disciplinary probation.

Probationary Period

Almost all contracts specify that a newly hired employee must undergo a probationary period to determine if he/she is suitable for the job. These periods usually range from thirty to ninety days, although some contracts have longer probationary periods. During the probationary period, the employee may be discharged without resort to the grievance and arbitration provision. In other words, the employee is "at will" during the probationary period. Naturally, statutory protections, such as nondiscrimination statutes, still protect a probationary employee, but the union contract will not. Similarly, an employer could not discharge a probationary employee for his/her union activity and escape liability under Section 8(a)(3) merely because the employee was probationary.

Probationary employees do not become members of the union until their probationary period is completed. Seniority is not accumulated during the probationary period, although most contracts provide that if the employee successfully completes the probationary period, his/her seniority will be made retroactive to the date of hire.

Most layoff provisions also provide that probationary employees will be the first to be laid off, even if their department or job classification is not affected by the layoff.

Leaves of Absence

Most contracts provide for leaves of absence for various reasons. They also will specify whether and to what extent the leaves will be paid and the impact of the leave on the employee's seniority. Common leaves include work-related injury, medical leave (nonwork related), bereavement leave, union business leave (to attend union conventions or to serve as a union employee for a period of time), and military leave.

The contracts leave provisions generally cannot deprive employees of leave rights they would have under law, either state or federal, unless the law in question allows for deviation in a collective bargaining agreement. In particular, the terms of the Family Medical Leave Act and the Uniformed Services Employment and Reemployment Rights Act must be observed.

Some contracts contain provisions requiring an employee to report in periodically during leave to advise the company of his/her status and expected return to work date. Contractual provisions also may stipulate that the employee will submit to a return to work physical examination and/or drug test if he/she has been gone for a specified period of time or based on the reasons for the leave.

Discipline and Discharge

Almost all labor contracts provide that management may discharge and discipline for "just cause." This may be worded a little differently depending on the contract. Some contracts, for instance, use the phrase "good and sufficient cause" or "good cause." It is all the same. The bottom line is that these simple phrases place a significant limitation on the right of management. Employees may no longer be disciplined and discharged at will. In the final analysis, just cause is whatever an arbitrator says it is.

It is difficult to briefly summarize this concept. Volumes have been written about the subject. "Just cause" stems from the concept of fairness, although it is not co-extensive with it. A discharge may be based on just cause, but is not necessarily fair and vice versa.

The following concepts are usually held to be a part of the just cause requirement:

- An employee must have notice of the rule, policy, standard, or prohibition that he/she is alleged to have violated.
- The rule, policy, standard, or prohibition must be a legitimate one based on business considerations.
- In most cases, the employee must receive a warning that his/her conduct/performance does not comply with the policy or standard (or expected behavior) and that further discipline up to and including discharge may result if improvement or change in behavior is not forthcoming; This is often known as *progressive discipline.* The idea behind progressive discipline is to correct behavior or performance problems. It connotes increasingly severe forms of discipline if the previous form was not successful in correcting the behavior. A common progressive discipline format is verbal warning, written warning, suspension without pay, and discharge.
- Serious offenses, such as theft, fighting on the job, falsification of documents and the like, usually do not require progressive discipline.
- The employer must prove that the employee, in fact, did commit the offense or engage in the behavior complained of.
- The employer must give the employee a chance to tell his/her side of the story before making a decision. This will almost always involve a meeting where the employee is represented by a union steward or perhaps the business agent. The employee should be able to suggest witnesses or other items that are exculpatory or mitigating. This concept is often referred to as *industrial due process,* named after the right of criminal suspects to have counsel, conduct a defense in a court of law, etc.
- The discipline imposed must be reasonable in light of the offense committed.
- The employer may not discriminate in the imposition of discipline without good reason. In other words, like cases should usually be treated alike. Put another way, just cause requires that an employer be consistent in meting out

discipline. For instance, firing one employee for sleeping on the job, but suspending without pay another employee who commits the same offense might violate this concept unless the employer had a nonarbitrary reason for differentiating between the two employees. For example, the suspended employee might have had much more seniority or the discharged employee might have committed the offense before and this was the second offense.

Many contracts will contain a provision specifying that management will be "deemed" to have just cause to discharge in the case of certain offenses. These will usually be the more serious offenses, such as those mentioned above. This does not, however, relieve the employer of the requirements to prove that the employee committed the offense, to impose consistent discipline, or to provide industrial due process. The main impact of this clause is to remove from the arbitrator the power to mitigate the punishment once the employee is proved to have committed the offense. Different arbitrators have different views on the extent to which such clauses impact their otherwise well recognized power to reduce penalties.

Some contracts spell out the progressive discipline procedure. That is, they specifically require verbal and written warnings be given before moving to more serious discipline. Many contracts provide that discipline imposed say, for instance, one year ago, will not be considered in the progressive disciplinary process. Other contracts state that the subsequent offense must be similar in nature to the earlier offense in order to progress to a more serious step of discipline. For instance, an employee who receives a warning for absenteeism and then commits an unrelated offense (damage to equipment, for example) would not be eligible for the next step of the process.

Some disciplinary policies deal with absenteeism separately. Two approaches are typical: either a modification of the progressive disciplinary system or a "no fault" system.

The first approach usually has a progressive system for absences and tardiness. The first offense will be a verbal warning and so on. Usually, the employee who has maintained perfect attendance for a certain amount of time will get a "fresh start," with the earlier discipline "dropping off" the employee's record.

Because there are so many reasons an employee may be absent, some being more justified than others, this first approach usually makes exceptions for certain absences, such as those for medical reasons assuming proper documentation (e.g., a doctor's excuse) is presented. Naturally, absences authorized under the employer's leave programs would not count against the employee. However, what about the myriad excuses employers inevitably get for absences?

My car wouldn't start.
The electricity went off and my alarm clock didn't work.
I had to take my child to the hospital.
I had to go take care of my sick brother.

I was delayed at the train crossing.
The bus was behind schedule.

These are usually dealt with on a case-by-case basis. Naturally, the possibility of inconsistent discipline or application of the attendance rules is high, especially when deciding if an absence is excused is left up to the individual supervisor. These headaches are usually why many employers adopt the "no fault" system.

The no fault system is usually based on points or occurrences. An absence of a full day is worth a point, for instance. Coming in late to work is ¼ point and so on. The way the points are set up varies greatly. The main concept, however, is that it doesn't matter what your excuse is; you get points assessed and if you get over a certain amount, you are fired. Up to that point, you will have a job. Despite the no fault nature of the system, even these programs usually make exceptions. Naturally, they cannot deprive employees of statutory rights under laws, such as the Family Medical Leave Act or the military service reemployment rights law. Second, a common exception is made for work-related injuries. Indeed, in many states, it is unlawful to terminate an employee while on a work-related injury absence. Third, medical-related absences are either excused or only charged as one point, assuming documentation is presented.

Many no-fault policies provide that employees must be given a notice every time they incur a point, to include a summary of how many points they have accumulated. Usually the time period involved is twelve months. When an employee has perfect attendance for a specified period of time, his/her previous points are voided, either in whole or in part.

As with most such systems, there are all sorts of ways to "play games" with a point system. Many employees will have perfect attendance for a lengthy period of time and then take a "points vacation," knowing that they have the "luxury" of incurring a few points. Naturally, these employees risk that they will get sick later on or otherwise will need to be absent and will not have sufficient points left to accommodate their need to be gone.

Drug Testing Programs

Many labor agreements contain some form of drug testing procedure. You also must take state law into account when formulating a drug testing program. State drug testing laws range from those states having no law at all to those with highly restrictive statutes. Furthermore, some employees, such as truck drivers, pipeline operators, and similar occupations, must be drug tested under federal law.

Most policies specify that illegal drug use, sale, possession, etc. are prohibited and violation of the policy is grounds for disciplinary action and/or discharge. The illegal drugs prohibited are named and a cut-off score is established for when a test will be deemed positive. Many policies also prohibit use of prescription medication by those for whom the medicine was not prescribed.

The different occasions for testing are usually spelled out in the contract. Most common forms of testing are applicant testing, postaccident testing, reasonable suspicion testing (when you have a reason to believe someone is under the influence of a drug, e.g., slurred speech, staggering, bizarre behavior, etc.), return to duty testing, and postrehabilitation follow-up testing (an employee who was on a drug rehabilitation program may be subject to unannounced testing), and random testing. Most unions do not like random testing and will not agree to it. Random testing is where names are put into a computer or literally into a hat and a few are selected for testing. Although random testing is a good deterrent, it is not found that often in labor agreements.

The drug testing provision will specify as well what happens if an employee does test positive for drugs. Unlike most policies of nonunion employers, drug testing programs in a unionized setting usually require the employee to get a "second chance" upon testing positive for the first time. This second chance will usually involve some type of rehabilitation program coupled with a "last chance" agreement that specifies that the employee will be terminated immediately if he/she tests positive a second time (within a designated time frame, such as one year) or otherwise violates the terms of the last chance letter.

Sometimes, these policies will include alcohol in the substances that may be tested. They will provide, on occasion, for the employee who tests positive for a prohibited substance to challenge the result by having another laboratory test the sample. Chain of custody and other protections against mishandling or safeguards of the integrity of the process are often spelled out in the contract provision regarding drug testing.

Protection of Bargaining Unit Work

Naturally, the labor contract would not be worth much to the union or the employees if the employer could have other people outside the bargaining unit perform bargaining unit work. Nevertheless, there may be times when it is more efficient for the employer to do so. At other times, the employer may have no other choice but to do so. These competing considerations usually result in several different provisions in the contract. These clauses are different in scope, but they all have as their object the preservation of bargaining unit work and the right of unit members to perform such work.

Subcontracting Clauses

The ability of the employer to subcontract work is often hotly debated. Many times such ability will be reserved to management in the management rights clause of the labor contract. More often than not, however, there will be a specific clause containing some restrictions on management. Some clauses allow management to subcontract whenever it is more economical or expedient to do so. Others would allow subcontracting only when unit employees do not have sufficient expertise to perform the work or perhaps when unit employees are so busy there is no way the employer can meet customer demands unless it subcontracts some of the work. Unions are sometimes suspicious that the employer is subcontracting to "erode the bargaining unit," i.e., slowly diminish the number of employees in the unit. Most arbitrators hold that if it can be shown that an employer was subcontracting work with the specific purpose to erode the unit, then the employer is in violation of the agreement for an illicit motive, even if the subcontracting clause otherwise would have allowed the employer to subcontract in a given situation.

Supervisors Performing Bargaining Unit Work

Most contracts prohibit supervisors from performing bargaining unit work except in emergency situations or when training new employees. Some contracts allow supervisors to perform unit work when no other qualified employee is available (this is often characterized as an "emergency").

Use of Temporary Employees

The business world has seen increasing use of temporary employees in all job categories from unskilled labor to professional positions, such as engineers or accountants. In the realm of labor agreements, however, use of temporary employees is severely restricted in most cases. The reason is obvious. If an employer can use nonunion temporary employees at will, why would it want to hire more union workers or keep as many as it already has? Contracts take different approaches on limiting temporaries. Some ban them altogether. Others limit the number that can be employed at any one time and/or limit the time period they can be employed. Others provide that if a temporary employee works over a certain amount of time that employee must be made a regular employee and, therefore, he/she would become a member of the bargaining unit.

In some cases, contracts provide for a maximum ratio between temporary employees and regular, union-represented employees.

Wages and Benefits

The contract will specify the wage rate applicable to each classification as well as what benefits are available to employees. Typically, the wage rate will increase on each anniversary of the contract during its term. Premium pay for overtime, shift work, or working on weekends or holidays also may be provided. Minimum pay for reporting for scheduled work and work not being available is a common feature. Premium pay for being called from home to work is usually provided. Programs such as health insurance, life insurance, and pension plans usually will not be set forth in the collective bargaining agreement in their entireties. Instead, a reference will be made to them along with restrictions on the employer's ability to change insurers or the specifics of benefits without union approval.

Vacations and holidays will be the subject of several paragraphs. There will be some type of formula for calculating how much vacation an employee may take in a year, e.g., five years service entitles the employee to three weeks of vacation and so on. Many contracts provide whether or not an employee can carry over unused vacation from one year to another. If carryover is allowed, there is usually a maximum amount of vacation that can be accrued. Some contracts allow employees to "cash in" unused vacation. The method of accrual is usually specified as so many days or hours per month. There is usually a restriction on when new employees will be eligible to take vacation. Probationary employees usually are ineligible to take vacation.

Contracts also may allow employees to take vacations in increments of less than a week at a time, such as a day or partial day. Conversely, the contract also may limit the maximum amount of vacation that may be taken at a time, such as three weeks. The agreement usually specifies how and when employees can request vacation and may provide what rights management has to deny vacation if operational needs dictate or if a number of employees have asked for vacation over the same time period. Some employers who have seasonal businesses limit vacations during the busy time of year.

Some employers shut down their entire operations for a week at a given time of year in order to perform maintenance or for some other reason. Contracts involving such employers will usually specify whether employees must use a week of vacation during this shut down period or if they can take the time as unpaid leave and save the vacation time for later use.

The rate of pay for vacation time is also specified. It is usually couched in terms of one or more weeks of base pay, exclusive of overtime.

Holidays are dealt with somewhere in the contract as well, usually in a separate provision. All contracts will specify what days are considered holidays. An employee is usually paid his/her daily rate of pay for being off on the holiday. In order to deter employees from "stretching" the holiday, it is usually required that an employee work his/her normally scheduled shift before and after the holiday. Employees who are required to work on a holiday will be given premium pay, usually double or triple time. The precise amount may depend on the holiday worked.

Also, the contract will deal with the situation that arises when a holiday falls during an employee's vacation or when he/she is otherwise off work.

Hours of Work

This basic provision is found in nearly all labor contracts. This is the part of the agreement that will specify the normal hours of work, starting and ending times of shifts, and the employer's ability (or lack thereof) to change these items. Usually overtime rules are specified. Most union contracts provide for overtime at the rate of time and one-half for any hours worked in excess of the normal daily schedule, regardless of how many hours are worked within a work week. Premium pay is often required for work on weekends. Indeed, some contracts limit the amount of weekend work or overtime unless it is voluntary on the part of the employee.

Shift differential is a common feature in those facilities working more than one shift. Employees held beyond their shift into the next also may receive shift differential in addition to overtime (which would probably include the shift differential in the regular rate).

Incentive Programs

Some contracts contain production bonuses or other incentive arrangements. Most unions prefer systems whereby entitlement to the bonus can be measured as objectively as possible, e.g., feet of pipe shipped out the door or something based on a percentage of a net profit. Unions ordinarily will have access to those employer records necessary to verify that the bonuses or incentive program was properly administered in accordance with the contract.

Reopener Provisions

These provisions allow the contract to be "reopened" at a particular time in order that the parties may renegotiate one or more provisions. Negotiations are limited to those specified. Other parts of the contract remain in effect. Wages are the most common subject of reopeners. Sometimes these provisions are inserted because of volatile economic times. In any event, the danger of such clauses is if the parties cannot come to agreement on the reopened subject, the union can usually strike. Management could lock out. A few contracts call for the dispute to be submitted to binding arbitration. Thus, if a three-year contract had a reopener for wages after the first year, it is really a one-year contract for purposes of wages and the no strike/no lockout clause. Most management personnel do not like reopeners and avoid them whenever possible.

Zipper Clause

These clauses "zip up" the contract and are designed to prevent one of the parties from trying to bargain about something during the term of the contract. They are sometimes viewed as a waiver of the union's right to bargain. The Labor Board has changed position several times on the effectiveness of a zipper clause and the reviewing federal appeals courts also have gone in different directions. As with any other clause, the effectiveness of a zipper clause will depend on how well it is written. A sample may be found in Appendix 5.

Successorship Clause

Unions like to get these clauses whenever they can. To understand why, a short discussion of the "law of successorship" is in order. When one company buys the assets of another company and continues the business, it is known as a successor. If the selling company has a union contract, the buying company does not have to honor that contract. It must, however, recognize the union that continues to be the bargaining agent of the employees. In this event, the successor employer must negotiate a new contract with the union, assuming it does not want to honor the old contract (which it is free to do if the union is in agreement). Furthermore, if a majority of the buying company's employees are not employees of the old company, the buyer is not deemed a successor at all and has no obligation whatsoever. Some unscrupulous companies intentionally do not hire the employees of the selling company in order to avoid the obligation of being a successor. This action risks being found guilty of an unfair labor practice because it is a violation of the Act to refuse to hire someone because of his/her union affiliation.

A successorship clause in a labor agreement changes these rules. Basically, this provision obligates the company, in the event of a sale of its assets, to require (as a condition of sale) that the buying company honor the union contract in place at the time. Companies often balk at this because it might interfere with their ability to sell the company. In any event, there is quite a bit of pressure placed on local union leaders by the international union organization to obtain such clauses.

From the employees' point of view, such provisions are beneficial because a sale of the company is much less likely to lead to job loss or to major changes in working conditions. Naturally, unions will be able to keep the bargaining unit and be recognized by the new company as the exclusive bargaining agent of the unit employees.

If the sale is of the stock of the company, the new employer is essentially the same as the old company and all labor arrangements will continue.

Amendment Procedure

Most contracts spell out how the parties may mutually agree to amend the contract. Typically, the amendment must be in writing and signed by authorized representatives of both parties in order for it to be effective.

Provisions Relating to the Conduct of Union Business

Many contracts will specify what rights stewards and other union officials have while investigating grievances and the like. They also will specify what right of access the union business agent has to the facility and will usually contain some requirement that the business agent give notice of his/her intent to visit and other stipulations limiting his/her ability to roam about the facility once present. If not already covered in the leave of absence section, this section will usually specify when union employees may take leave to attend union conventions, union training, conduct union business, etc. Payment or nonpayment for time spent during the workday conducting union business is dealt with in most contracts as well.

Termination of the Agreement

This is another trap for the unwary. Most agreements require a certain amount of notice from one party to the other that there is a desire to negotiate a renewal agreement. Typically, agreements provide that if notice is not given, the contract automatically renews for another year. These notice requirements may or may not coincide with the notice requirements of Section 8(d) of the Act. If they do not, you must comply with both Section 8(d) and the notice provisions in the agreement.

Chapter 6

Grievances

What Is a Grievance?

Grievances are usually defined as a dispute between the union and the company over the application of the contract. Put another way, most grievances involve the union claiming the company has violated a term of the collective bargaining agreement. A few contracts allow the company to file a grievance, but this is not a recommended practice. Management should be able to act as it sees fit, and not be required to file a grievance every time it believes the union or an employee is doing something wrong. Following the old saying that "management acts and the union reacts" is the best way to conduct labor relations. After all, the company is in charge of the workplace. The union and the company are not co-employers.

Most grievances are raised by individual employees, but it is the union that decides whether grievances will be filed and, if so, how far they will be processed in the grievance system and, most importantly, whether they will be taken all the way to arbitration. A detailed discussion of the union's legal duty to its members is beyond the scope of this book. Suffice it to say, however, that a union is under no obligation to accept every grievance or to take every grievance to arbitration. The union's duty is to make a reasonable investigation of the matter and to refrain from acting in an arbitrary or discriminatory manner.

Thus, although an employee may feel strongly that he or she was wronged by the company, it is up to the union in the ultimate analysis as to how the matter will be handled.

Examples of Grievances

Most grievances fall into one of two categories: (1) discipline and discharge, and (2) contract terms violations.

If an employee is terminated or suspended, the contract usually requires it be for just cause. This concept has been discussed in Chapter 5, p.103. If the union feels that the disciplinary action is not supported by just cause, a grievance may be filed. The grievance will usually seek to restore the employee to the place he/she would have been but for the faulty discipline/discharge. Grievances merely seek "make whole" relief. There is no provision for punitive damages or damages for pain and suffering similar to that found in courts of law.

The other type of grievance concerns an allegation that management has violated some nondisciplinary provision of the contract. For instance, the union may claim that management is not properly applying the provisions of the seniority provision of the contract by failing to promote the most senior, qualified employee to a particular job. There may be a dispute over how overtime is calculated in a given situation. These grievances may involve only one employee or the entire bargaining unit.

Grievance Procedures

Grievance procedures may be different in their details, but they have several things in common.

First, there are the requirements that must be met for filing a grievance. Typically, the grievance must relate to an alleged breach of the collective bargaining agreement to include the just cause requirements for discipline and discharge.

The grievance must be reduced to a written form at some point in the procedure. Some agreements require the grievance to state the article(s) of the contract alleged to have been violated and that an authorized union official (or, in some cases, an employee and the union official) must sign the grievance.

The grievance must be presented within a certain period of time after the alleged violation arose or is discovered by the union. Usually this time period is short, often ten calendar days or five business days. The consequences for failing to file on time are less certain. It depends on whether the contract specifies such consequences and/or whether the union has some good excuse for the late filing.

The grievance must be presented to a management official designated by the contract.

Second, once the grievance is filed, it is presented to the official as described above. This is known as Step 1 of the procedure. Almost all grievance procedures have two or more steps. The subsequent steps usually involve different decision makers on the company's side and sometimes on the union's as well. For instance, the first step may involve the foreman who is the supervisor of the employee involved in the grievance. The second step may involve the plant superintendent. The third step may involve the company's vice president for human resources. On the union's side, the first step may involve the steward. The second step also might involve the steward and the union business agent. The third step will usually involve the business agent, or, in some cases, his/her superior.

Third, management usually has a certain amount of time to render a decision at each step of the process. Once again, the time limit is usually short, maybe five days or even less. The consequences of management's failure to respond within the designated time frame is usually that the grievance is advanced to the next step. In a few agreements, the penalty for management delay is that the grievance is considered granted. Usually, management's decision is required to be in writing.

Fourth, if the union is dissatisfied with management's response, it must affirmatively do something to advance the grievance to the next step of the process. This is usually a simple written statement expressing the desire to go forward. Usually, the time limit for the union to make this decision is short. If it delays, it risks forfeiting the grievance under the provisions of many labor agreements.

Fifth, the grievance may be settled at any stage of the process. Just because a grievance is filed does not mean it must go through all of the steps to be settled. In fact, many studies show that most grievances are settled at the first or second step. In my opinion, this is a sign of a healthy relationship between union and management.

Sixth, as we have noted, the time limits are short. One of the key concepts of a grievance procedure is to resolve disputes quickly and efficiently. This is good for both company and union.

Seventh, any settlement of the grievance is based on mutual agreement of company and union. If the grievance is not resolved to the satisfaction of the union, it may either move forward to the next step or withdraw the grievance. Usually, such withdrawals are said to be "without prejudice." This means the union is not admitting its arguments are invalid, just that "it is not going to fight this one." It may make the same argument on another occasion.

Eighth, if, at the end of the grievance procedure the matter is not settled or dropped, the union may move the issue to binding arbitration by a third party neutral. We will discuss the arbitration process in more detail below.

The Supervisor's Role in the Grievance Procedure

Most likely a supervisor's role will be one or more (and perhaps all) of the following:

- Decision maker
- Investigator
- Witness

As a decision maker, you may be the individual assigned to answer the grievance at one of the steps of the procedure. Naturally, before you make any decisions you must first investigate the grievance, which will be discussed below.

Typically, once you have accumulated the necessary facts and information, you will give your answer to the grievance in writing. It is usually not necessary to go into great detail in your written answer. You must be very careful what you write. For instance, if you set forth a list of reasons why you denied the grievance, what happens if one turns out not to be factually supported at a subsequent arbitration. What if you leave out a reason inadvertently that the company needs to rely on in an arbitration? Does this mean that the decision must be overturned? Why put yourself in this position? It is usually enough to say the grievance is denied because investigation revealed the company did not violate the contract.

This does not mean you should not discuss the reasons for your decision with the appropriate union official and/or the employee. It is often difficult to encapsulate the entire reasoning process in a written document. Don't set this difficult task for yourself. You are not required to by the contract or law.

Also, ensure that your decision is rendered in a timely manner under the contract. If you need more time, ask your union counterpart. If he or she agrees, get it in writing and expect to do the same thing for him/her in the future if the union needs more time.

Make sure you consult with appropriate officials before making a decision and announcing it to the union. In particular, you need to ensure that the discipline or other issue involved is being handled consistently with prior discipline or other company interpretation of the contract.

Document the meeting with the union where you announce your decision (assuming it is done in a meeting; most contracts do not require this). Also, any meeting with the employee grievant must include union representation.

Above all, if the contract entrusts to your judgment a decision in a step of the grievance process, take this obligation seriously. You must be fair, consistent with your obligations to follow the contract. On the other hand, don't give into the union thinking that you are going to be popular, because you won't. You will be viewed as a pushover. It's just like any other business decision you make. You have to "call it like you see it and let the chips fall where they may."

Investigating a Grievance

Let's say that an employee has been discharged for sleeping on the job. The union has filed a grievance on his behalf, claiming the employee was not asleep.

Naturally, a good place for you to start is interviewing the employees who saw the individual sleeping. Chances are they have already made out statements to support the decision to discharge and you should review these statements. However, you should also interview the individuals concerned.

As with any eyewitness testimony, you should determine whether or not these people were actually in a position to observe the event. If there is more than one eyewitness, are their stories consistent? You should probe for whether there may be other explanations for what they thought was an employee sleeping. Was the employee merely resting his eyes at his desk? Or was he lying down on a makeshift bed of cardboard boxes in the back room?

You also should consider whether the eyewitness has a motive to harm the grievant. Perhaps the grievant received a promotion that the witness thought he/she should have had.

Go over the sequence of events with the witness, especially the timing. In the case of the example at hand (sleeping on the job), I would want to know how long the witness actually observed the employee "sleeping." Was the observation just after lunch, at a time when the employee may have fallen asleep inadvertently (most arbitrators will make a distinction between "intentional" sleeping and nodding off despite trying to stay awake).

I might also want to know if the employee alleges he was taking medication that made him drowsy and whether this was prescribed by a doctor. Although this might raise some questions under the Americans with Disabilities Act and some state disability laws, I believe an inquiry under these circumstances is justified, especially if the employee raises this as a defense. I would ask the employee for a copy of the prescription.

Another area of inquiry might be to ask others if the employee has been observed sleeping before. His/her co-workers may be reluctant to talk to you. Union workers often "stick together" when it comes to such matters. Some may demand to have a union steward there when they are interviewed. Fact witnesses (e.g. those who observed acts of one discharged employee) being interviewed have no legal right to the presence of a steward unless the contract or past practice (a concept to be discussed later) allows for his. Nevertheless, I usually would allow the union steward to be present so long as he/she does not interfere with my questions or advise the employee not to answer a legitimate question. After all, we have nothing to hide.

I would next review the employee's personnel file to determine the quality of his/her service to the company and to determine if there are any instances of prior misconduct, especially if they are similar or the same as the one being investigated. This review goes not to the question of whether the employee is guilty, but to whether the penalty should be mitigated. A long history of good service to the company may influence you to reduce the penalty. You might as well consider it at this point because an arbitrator will later, if it goes that far.

As mentioned above, you also need to consider whether there have been other instances of sleeping on the job by other employees. What happened to them? What were the facts? How similar are they to the facts in the case at hand?

At some point in this process, usually after you have done most of the investigation, you should give the union and/or employee a chance to be confronted with this evidence and an opportunity to respond. This may require you to reveal the names of informants and witnesses. I realize this puts you in a difficult position, but put yourself in the union's place. How can it respond to anonymous charges of misconduct?

The union and/or employee may suggest additional witnesses to interview or documents to review. You should take these suggestions seriously and follow up.

Keep an open mind. If the union's evidence causes you to doubt your case, you may wish to consider some type of settlement or even reversing the discipline. If you have doubts about your case, an arbitrator probably will too. Now, I am talking about **serious doubts,** not theoretical possibilities or union "smoke and mirrors." I have never seen a case but what the union could ostensibly poke a hole here and there. No case is perfect. Life is just not that way. If, after conducting your investigation, you have no substantial doubt about the discipline imposed or other decision of management, you should uphold the company's decision.

Some Miscellaneous Points about Grievances

- Don't let the union "expand" the grievance. For instance, the grievance will start out with a claim that the company is not paying correct overtime for employees held over after their shifts. Then, at a later stage of the process, the grievance is modified to include overtime for employees called in early to begin their shift. You do not have to accept this type of expansion of the grievance. You need to deal with one issue at a time. If you do not, the union may dump anything it can think of into the grievance.
- If the union claims it has exculpatory evidence, ask them to produce it. If the union doesn't, and tries to introduce it at an arbitration hearing later on, the arbitrator may not consider it if the company objects.
- Many times a union agent will approach you in an attempt to settle a controversy informally, without filing a grievance. You should welcome such opportunities, although it is not always possible to settle the matter short of a grievance. Just make sure you have all the facts you need and have checked with appropriate officials before you enter into any resolution. It will be binding on you, at least as to the case in question.
- Be businesslike and keep your cool. Things could be worse. If it were not for the grievance and arbitration procedure, the union could strike every time the company did something it didn't like. This is the way labor relations are conducted in some countries. Let's be thankful it's not that way here. Look at the grievance process as an orderly way to resolve differences and prevent misunderstandings.
- Unfortunately, sometimes unions may misuse the grievance procedure. This is especially likely to happen at contract negotiation time. The purpose of this is usually to gain advantage at the bargaining table or to keep the company off balance. On other occasions, the union will hope that numerous grievances can get from the employer what it could not get at the bargaining table. It may hope the company will tire of having to deal with these grievances or that it can convince an arbitrator to decide in its favor.

Chapter 7

Labor Arbitration

What Is Labor Arbitration?

Labor arbitration involves the submission of a dispute pertaining to the collective bargaining agreement to a neutral third party who renders a decision that is final and binding. In these days of alternative dispute resolution, I often point out to my colleagues in the bar that we have had alternative dispute resolution in the labor management arena for seventy years or more. Although it has its faults, labor arbitration has proved itself again and again as being the best way to resolve most disputes over the interpretation and application of the collective bargaining agreement.

The Legal Status of Labor Arbitration

The legal status of labor arbitration was established by the U.S. Supreme Court in a group of cases referred to as the "Steelworkers Trilogy" in the early 1960s. All of these cases involved the Steelworkers union and thus the name.*

Without trying to present a lengthy legal discussion of these cases, we can distill the holdings to the following crucial points:

- There is a national policy in favor of labor arbitration. It directly contributes to industrial peace and is the *quid pro quo* for a pledge by the union not to strike during the term of the agreement.

---

* United Steelworkers v. American Manufacturing Co., 363 U.S. 564 (1960); United Steelworkers v. Warrior & Gulf Navigation Co., 363 U.S. 574 (1960); United Steelworkers v. Enterprise Wheel & Car Corp., 363 U.S. 593 (1960).

■ Arbitration clauses should be construed broadly. Courts will find most disputes to be subject to labor arbitration (although this may vary depending on how the arbitration language in the contract is drafted).
■ The fact that the company thinks a dispute is utterly without merit (and can prove it) is not grounds to refuse arbitration. If the dispute arises under a provision of the agreement, it is arbitrable.
■ The arbitrator's decision will not be overturned unless it can be shown he/she did not base the award on the provisions of the contract or was otherwise biased for one side. An arbitrator is not allowed to dispense his/her "own brand of industrial justice," but must interpret the parties agreement. The arbitrator derives his/her power from the parties themselves and from their contract.

In an earlier decision, the Supreme Court noted that federal law would apply to arbitration disputes, not state law.* Many state courts were distrustful of labor arbitration years ago and would not uphold the legitimacy of arbitration provisions in labor contracts. The Supreme Court made it clear that state courts had no power to apply state law to arbitration disputes with regard to employees who were covered by the National Labor Relations Act.

Later Supreme Court cases have added even more potency to the concept of labor arbitration. For instance, it is now clear that a dispute that arises when the labor agreement is in effect must be arbitrated if the union so desires even though the old contract that created the arbitration duty has expired. Another case held that the public policy in favor of arbitration was so strong that it required an arbitrator's decision to be upheld who ordered an employee who was using drugs reinstated to his job.† That is, the public policy in favor of having a drug-free workplace was outweighed by the policy in favor of labor arbitration.

In more recent years, the Supreme Court has upheld arbitration provisions in employment agreements in companies where no unions were involved. Once again, the High Court based its decision on the strong public policy in favor of informal, inexpensive, speedy resolution of disputes that arbitration provides (at least in comparison to law suits).‡

How Is an Arbitrator Selected?

The parties can specify any method they desire in the collective bargaining agreement. Most parties to labor agreements obtain their arbitrators from one of two agencies: the Federal Mediation and Conciliation Service (FMCS) or the American

---

* Textile Workers Union v. Lincoln Mills, 353 U.S. 448 (1957).
† United Paperworkers International Union, AFL-CIO v. Misco, Inc., 484 U.S. 29 (1987).
‡ EEOC v. Waffle House, Inc., 534 U.S. 279 (2002).

Arbitration Association (AAA). There are some regional agencies that provide arbitrators to parties within the local area. There are also some arrangements where the company and the union appoint a "permanent panel" of arbitrators who hear cases in a rotating order.

In the case of the FMCS, AAA, and most regional/local agencies, the parties will request a panel of arbitrators. The agency, in turn, will furnish a panel with an odd number of names, usually seven, but it could be five or nine. The parties (union and company) will alternate striking names from the panel until only one name is left. That person is the arbitrator.

Many "old hands" feel that the party who strikes first is at a disadvantage because it is the other party who will get to select the arbitrator from the remaining two names. I'm not so sure that there is much of an advantage here. Nevertheless, it is advisable to come up with some system on who strikes first. A lot of companies rotate, that is, the union will strike first in grievance A, but the company will strike first when the next grievance comes along. Others flip a coin. A few collective bargaining agreements specify who will strike first.

The types of people on the panels are often professors, consultants, lawyers, or people who do nothing but arbitrate cases. Many of these people will often be willing to serve as mediators. They must subscribe to a code of professional responsibility set forth by the National Academy of Arbitrators. Some have union backgrounds. Some have worked in management capacities. Some have been on both union and management sides. Others have been in a strictly neutral capacity. For instance, I notice many retired EEOC (Equal Employment Opportunity Commission) or NLRB (National Labor Relations Board) officials on the panels.

Researching an Arbitrator

I have always spent a great deal of time researching the panel of arbitrators before striking names. Remember the Steelworkers Trilogy? An arbitrator's decision is hard to overturn. You are truly putting all your eggs in one basket with the arbitrator, and it pays to find out which arbitrators on the panel may be more favorable to your case.

Some people automatically strike law professors or former union officials. This is a mistake. I prefer to look at the reported decisions of these people, particularly ones that involved disputes similar to the one at hand. I also like to talk to colleagues who may know the individuals concerned, especially those who reside in the same local area as the arbitrator. Many of the people on your panel will be from other states, and it is often helpful to talk to someone who may have more knowledge of the person's background and record as an arbitrator.

There are also private companies who collect information about arbitrators and who, for a fee, will share that information with you. I have found these services to be useful, but only as a supplement to my own investigation described above.

Preparing for a Labor Arbitration Hearing

You may be tasked with presenting the company's case at the hearing or assisting those who do. Either way, it is important to understand how to get ready for an arbitration hearing.

As with most other important things in the business world, preparation can make the difference between success and failure. Not all cases will require the same amount of preparation. A one-witness case will not take as long as a case where there are numerous witnesses or highly technical issues involved in the grievance. In any event, one must give preparation the time it deserves in each case.

Here are some preparation pointers I have found useful:

- Review the grievance; make sure you understand what the union is saying the company did wrong.
- Review the *entire* collective bargaining agreement. Even though the grievance may involve only one article of the agreement, it may be possible that other articles will help the arbitrator interpret the article in question. Don't forget to determine if there are any side letters or memoranda of understanding that may bear on the case.
- Determine what individuals may have relevant information. This usually will be apparent from witness statements and other documents generated during the discharge procedures or during the grievance processing.
- Interview these potential witnesses *personally* and determine which will actually be called at the hearing. If any witnesses are no longer with the company, ask the arbitrator to issue a subpoena to that person. Your company's legal advisor can help you with this. It is very important that you select witnesses with first-hand knowledge of the facts. That is, avoid witnesses who can testify only from hearsay, what other people told them. Although the rules of evidence do not apply, some arbitrators will not accept hearsay evidence or else they will give it very little weight. This does not apply to statements of the grievant or union officials. These statements are not considered to be hearsay in most instances. Stress with each witness that he/she should not discuss his/her upcoming testimony with anyone and that, after he/she has testified, he/she should not discuss his/her testimony with other witnesses who have not yet testified.
- Determine what documents will be presented to the arbitrator as exhibits. Although the rules of evidence do not apply at the hearing, each exhibit should be "sponsored" or explained by a witness, either a company witness or a union witness. Determine which person will sponsor a given document. Have a "plan B," especially in the case of a union witness who does not show up at the hearing.
- Put your exhibits in the order you think they will come in at the hearing. Make sufficient copies for the arbitrator, the witness, and the union

representative and place them in separate files. Order the files in the same order you believe the exhibit copies they contain will come in at the hearing.

■ Some exhibits will be marked as joint exhibits and not need a sponsor. These usually include the labor agreement, the grievance, and the answer to the grievance. There may be others depending on the case.

■ Outline the questions you want to ask your witnesses. Sit down with the witness and go over these questions and make sure you know what he/she is going to say. Don't put words in his/her mouth. If he/she says things that hurt your case, consider not calling him/her. Now is the time to find out rather than at the hearing.

■ Acquaint your witnesses with the cross-examination questions they are likely to encounter. Go over with them the tips for witnesses, which appear in Appendix 11.

■ Outline the areas of cross examination for union witnesses who may be called. There may be statements from some of these people that were generated during the grievance investigation or in the discharge decision-making process. Statements also may have been generated during unemployment compensation proceedings. Have these statements handy at the hearing where you can easily retrieve them. If a witness says something different at the hearing compared to what he/she said in the statement, you may point this out to the arbitrator.

■ Prepare an opening statement for the arbitrator. This statement should be brief and nonargumentative. The purpose of the opening statement is to give the arbitrator a "mental framework" in which to put the evidence you and the union are about to present. Put another way, the opening statement tells the arbitrator what the case is about and what you expect the evidence to show. The statement itself is not evidence.

■ Prepare a hearing notebook with all of the above items placed therein in the same order they will come up during the hearing.

■ Consider whether you will have a court reporter present. Sometimes unions will object to this in which case you cannot have one there. In other situations, the union will split the cost with you and both sides will get a transcript. Most commonly, the union will not object to the reporter, but will not be willing to share in the cost. In this event, the union would not be entitled to a copy of the transcript because the company will pay the full cost. I usually find a transcript useful. First, the arbitrator gets a transcript, which is helpful to him/her. Second, it is of great assistance in preparing the posthearing brief (which will be discussed later).

■ Make sure all "housekeeping" arrangements have been made and confirmed, such as the room where the hearing will take place (often in a local hotel or motel), that the court reporter, if any, is confirmed, that the hotel staff knows how many people will be attending and can plan accordingly, that all witnesses know when and where the proceeding will be and what time they should arrive.

The Arbitration Hearing Itself

At the appointed time and place, hopefully you will have the full cast of characters assembled and ready to go. Most arbitrators conduct hearings informally, which should not be confused with casually. The parties are usually seated around a u-shaped table with the arbitrator at the head.

After informal introductions, the arbitrator will ask questions that usually cover preliminary matters with the party representatives. This discussion may take place on the record or off the record (and later summarized on the record) depending on the preference of the arbitrator.

These preliminary issues usually include:

- Whether the parties have agreed to a statement of the issue.
- Whether there are any "procedural issues" that might affect the arbitrator's ability to rule on the merits of the grievance, if proved. Examples might be an assertion by the company that the grievance was not filed in a timely manner. Another example would be that the dispute concerns issues that do not arise under the collective bargaining agreement (like the terms of a health insurance policy).
- If there are any joint exhibits that can be marked and introduced.
- Whether one party wishes to invoke the rule of sequestration (this means that all witnesses will be excluded from the hearing room except when they are testifying, except for the grievant and the company representative). (Sometimes the arbitrator will not bring up this issue and so it will be up to you to mention it. I do not always invoke the rule, especially if I have a lot of witnesses and I am going to present my case after the union.)
- Whether the parties have discussed settlement of the grievance and whether they wish to take some time before the hearing begins to discuss settlement. Not all arbitrators do this, but a few of them do. I have never understood why, because, by the time the case gets to arbitration, the parties have usually had numerous discussions about settlement. The fact that they are before the arbitrator usually means that settlement talks have failed.

Once these preliminary matters are finished, the parties proceed to give opening statements to the arbitrator. The party who has the burden of proof goes first and the other party will follow or, he/she may reserve his/her opening statement until the presentation of his case.

Who has the burden of proof and, therefore, the burden of going first? The answer is that it depends on the nature of the grievance. In discharge and discipline cases, the company has the burden of proof. In contract violation cases, the union has the burden. There is rarely any dispute about this. If there is, the arbitrator will make the decision.

After opening statements, the party with the burden calls its witnesses who are then subject to cross examination by the other side. Sometimes the arbitrator will ask questions. Exhibits are identified and received into evidence by the arbitrator.

After the party with the burden is done calling its witnesses, it rests and it is the other side's turn to do the same thing.

Once the party without the burden is done, the party with the burden may call rebuttal witnesses if allowed by the arbitrator. The purpose of a rebuttal witness is not to rehash testimony already given, but to rebut specific allegations made by the witnesses called by the other side.

Once all evidence has been taken, the arbitrator will give the parties an opportunity to make closing statements or present posthearing briefs. If the parties choose to submit briefs, they will usually agree at that time to a due date for the briefs to be submitted to the arbitrator.

I usually opt to present a posthearing brief. This will give me an opportunity to review the transcript of the hearing, to reflect upon the evidence, and to make comment on it to the arbitrator. It also will allow me to point out weakness in the union's case and to cite specific parts of the transcript or exhibits in support of my position. It also gives me the opportunity to cite cases decided by other arbitrators involving similar issues. These cases are not binding on the arbitrator, but they may be persuasive, especially if the contract language involved in those cases is similar.

I usually divide my briefs into four parts:

1. Introduction
2. Summary of the facts
3. Argument (This is where I usually cite cases from other arbitrators.)
4. Conclusion

One tricky issue often encountered is whether to anticipate the arguments that the union will make in its brief and try to deal with them in your brief. If you do not, and the union raises the argument in its brief, you will have missed your only opportunity to address it. On the other hand, if you bring up an anticipated argument that the union does not raise, you may have done the union a favor by bringing up a point in the union's behalf that it did not think to bring up itself. I don't know of any advice I can give you here except that there are some arguments you know the union will make. Deal with them. As to the others, you must use you best judgment and make a choice as to whether or not to bring them up.

Expedited Arbitration

There is a procedure for an expedited arbitration under FMCS rules. This usually involves a streamlined presentation of evidence and no posthearing briefs. Sometimes the arbitrator will rule "from the bench," i.e., at the close of the hearing. I do not recommend these procedures. Although they do have the advantage of getting things over quickly, haste can sometimes make waste. Important subjects deserve a full hearing and all that goes with it. If the issue is not that important, maybe it should not be arbitrated.

Enforcement of Arbitration Awards

Most arbitration awards are respected by the company and union. Occasionally, however, one side or the other does not believe the award to be proper and will challenge it. There are two ways to do this. File a lawsuit in federal court to vacate the award or wait until the other side files a lawsuit asking the court to enforce the award. This litigation can be expensive and should only be undertaken in extreme situations where the arbitrator has gone beyond the contract, exhibited bias, or conducted a fundamentally unfair hearing.

The Relationship of the National Labor Relations Act to Arbitration

There are some grievances that also may constitute unfair labor practices. A common example would be where a union steward was fired allegedly because of his/her advocacy on behalf of the union. This would be a violation of the contract's just cause provision as well as a provision contained in many contracts prohibiting discrimination on the basis of union activities. It would be a violation of section 8(a)(3) of the National Labor Relations Act as well. How does the Labor Board handle such situations?

Usually, if an unfair labor practice charge is filed and there is also a pending grievance based on the same facts, the Board will defer to the arbitration process. That is, the Board will suspend proceedings until the arbitration has concluded. Once the arbitrator has rendered his/her award, the Board will examine the decision to ensure it adequately protected the employee's rights under the Act. If so, the Board will defer to the award of the arbitrator and the unfair labor practice proceedings will be terminated. This does not mean the arbitrator must have decided in favor of the grievant; merely that he/she heard the evidence and conducted a fair hearing that covered basically the same issues that would have been presented to the Board had the unfair labor practice proceeding gone forward.

The philosophy behind this practice of deferral is that the parties have chosen an arbitrator to hear a dispute. For the Board to hear the same dispute would constitute a misuse of taxpayer resources. If the Board is convinced the arbitrator did not perform his/her function, however, the Board will step in and decide the underlying unfair labor practice claim.

The Board will not defer, however, if the company is raising some procedural bar to the arbitration, such as a timeliness defense. The Board will ask the company to waive this defense as the price of deferral. If the company refuses, the Board will usually go ahead and process the charge.

Chapter 8

Unfair Labor Practice Proceedings

We have discussed (beginning in Chapter 3, in the section "Unfair Labor Practices") the various unfair labor practice charges that may be filed. Now we will briefly discuss the procedure by which these matters are resolved and what your role might be.

The Charge

Much like in the case of a labor election, the process starts with a single piece of paper filed with the Board: the unfair labor practice charge. An example of this document can be found in Appendix 10.

The Investigation

Although anyone can file a charge—union, employee, or company—we will couch our discussion in terms of the union filing a charge against the company, the most common scenario. After the charge is filed, the Board will notify the company of the filing of the charge and ask for a response within a set period of time. The Board will also ask the company to make witnesses available for interview by a Board agent on company premises who will take an affidavit from them. Whether you are willing to do this or not depends on numerous factors, but I usually cooperate.

The correspondence received from the Board may ask you to submit documents or allow the Board agent investigating the charge to view a portion of the work site involved in the case.

Management witnesses cannot be interviewed privately by the Board agent over the company's objections. A representative of the company (an attorney, perhaps) may attend the interviews of all management employees. On the other hand, the company has no right to have a representative present when the Board agent interviews nonmanagerial witnesses. Such witnesses should be instructed that they have the right to ask for a copy of their affidavit produced from the interview. Some employees will be willing to share this affidavit with you although you should not force them to comply.

Management witnesses should be encouraged to review their affidavits carefully. The company representative also has the right to review these documents. You should not be afraid to suggest changes. The Board agent is usually typing the affidavit him/herself, either as the witness is answering his/her questions or from notes. He/she is apt to summarize a group of sentences or thoughts in a way you do not feel is accurate. Do not hesitate to bring this to the agent's attention. Make sure that dates and names are correct. The affidavit is what the regional director and his/her staff will see when they are deciding whether to issue a complaint against the company. Additionally, if a complaint is issued and the matter proceeds to a hearing, the affidavit may be used to impeach the witness if he/she testifies in a manner inconsistent with the affidavit.

The Board agent is not limited to interviewing witnesses on company premises. They may contact such nonmanagerial people privately at their homes or elsewhere. The Board does have subpoena power, which may be enforced by a federal court.

The Board's investigation is not the only one that should be going on at this time. The company should be conducting its own investigation as well to determine if there is any merit in the unfair labor practice charge. You may play a role in this similar to that discussed in Chapter 7 (Labor Arbitration). On the other hand, the company may choose to employ legal counsel to advise them on this. Much of what counsel uncovers may be covered by the attorney–client privilege and/or the attorney work product privilege.

If the company is convinced that a wrong has been done, it is often better to settle the matter before a complaint is issued. Usually, the Board is more amenable to negotiation at this point than it is later after a complaint has been issued.

Generally, if you make witnesses available for interview, the Board agent will be a bit more forthcoming with the evidence the Board possesses to support the unfair labor practice charge. Otherwise, you will know precious little about what the Board has in its files. By this time, the Board has taken affidavits of the witnesses of the charging party (the union or an employee). Unlike in civil litigation, they do not have to produce these documents until the hearing, assuming there is one. Even then, they produce the affidavits shortly before you are due to cross examine the witness. If you are aware of at least some of the details of the evidence the Board has, you are in a much better position to rebut it during the investigation and, in consequence, improve your chances of avoiding a complaint.

I usually prepare a lengthy position statement outlining the company's position and accompany it with relevant documentation. If I am fairly sure a complaint will be issued no matter what I say, however, I may not be as forthcoming because it gives the general counsel (the lawyer who presents the government's case at an unfair labor practice hearing) a road map to my case.

Decision of the Regional Director

Once the investigation is complete, the investigative file will be transmitted to the regional director for action. He/she has four basic options in most cases:

1. Issue a complaint.
2. Refuse to issue a complaint and dismiss the charge.
3. Send the case back for more investigation.
4. Seek guidance from the Board's headquarters (usually an office called the Division of Advice).

Usually, one of the first two options is chosen.

If the regional director issues a complaint, the employer will be served with a copy of it. The employer must file a written answer to the complaint and raise any affirmative defenses it might have, such as timeliness, lack of jurisdiction, lack of employee status, etc. Failure to file a timely answer can result in the equivalent of a default judgment being entered.

At this point in time, officials from the general counsel's office will become involved. These are usually Board attorneys located at the regional office. Also by this time, it is fairly certain that the company will have employed attorneys to assist with the case.

The general counsel may issue a subpoena to the company to produce records and other data to be used at the hearing by the government. The company must decide whether it has any grounds to resist the subpoena.

If the regional director refuses to issue a complaint and dismisses the charge, the party filing the charge may essentially appeal this decision to the general counsel's office in Washington, D.C. The general counsel may either uphold the regional director, which would end the matter, or he/she may overturn the decision below and order the complaint to be issued.

The Unfair Labor Practice Hearing and Its Aftermath

An unfair labor practice hearing is usually held in the same general locale where the company and most of the witnesses will be located. The hearing is conducted by an administrative law judge who will be a lawyer and usually has been employed by the Board in various capacities for several years.

An unfair labor practice proceeding is much more formal than an arbitration. For the most part, for instance, the Federal Rules of Evidence apply.

Surprisingly however, the hearing follows the same basic framework as an arbitration proceeding. For instance, the judge will take care of preliminary matters, such as motions, etc. Then the government (which goes first) presents its opening statement, followed by the company. Following that, the government presents its evidence, followed by the company. Closing statements are usually followed by posthearing briefs.

The judge will render a written decision at a later date. His/her decision is subject to review by the Labor Board if requested by an aggrieved party. The Labor Board's decision, in turn, is subject to review by a United States Circuit Court of Appeals and then the U.S. Supreme Court.

Remedies That May Be Ordered by the Board

The judge may specify various remedies and these are subject as well to review by the Board. The Board has significant remedial authority, but it cannot award punitive damages, damages for emotional distress, and the like.

Much like an arbitrator, current law limits the Board to "make whole relief" in most cases. Back pay is a common remedy for those who have been wrongfully terminated. Usually, reinstatement is ordered even if it means a replacement employee must lose his/her job. Interest is usually added to such awards. The Board may also order lost benefits, such as vacation or pensions, to be restored along with seniority. In disciplinary cases, the employee's file is expunged of any record of the unlawful discipline or discharge. The Board also will order a notice to be posted for a specified period of time (usually sixty days) notifying employees that the employer has been found guilty of an unfair labor practice charge and reiterate the rights of employees under the National Labor Relations Act (NLRA).

Employees who have been discharged are under a duty to mitigate their damages, i.e., diligently seek suitable work and accept such work if offered. Failure to do so could result in a reduction of back pay or a total forfeiture of the same. Recently, the Board's rules on mitigation have become more employer friendly, basically requiring the employee to begin searching for work within two weeks of discharge. Whether this will remain the rule is yet to be seen.

If there is a dispute about a remedy ordered by the Board, the matter may be resolved in what is known as a compliance hearing, which is a relatively informal hearing before a compliance officer. The results of this hearing may be reviewed by the Board and, ultimately, the courts as well.

Once the Board has found a company guilty of an unfair labor practice, it is something that will be considered by the Board and used against you if you are ever charged again.

Chapter 9

Strikes and Lockouts

Strikes

Definition and Legal Basis for a Strike

Basically, a strike is a concerted work stoppage by employees. It is the most dramatic, if not the most potent tool in the union's arsenal of economic weapons. For hundreds of years, employees have withheld their labor as a way to force the boss to make concessions.

For employees in the private sector, the right to strike finds its origins in Section 7 of the National Labor Relations Act. As you may recall, this is the part of the law that allows employees to act collectively for their mutual aid and protection. A strike is such a collective action.

When May a Union Lawfully Strike?

As a general rule, the union may strike in three situations:

1. There is no collective bargaining agreement in place.
2. The collective bargaining agreement has expired.
3. The collective bargaining agreement does not contain a no-strike clause or it contains an exception to the no-strike clause (such as a reopener or lack of a ban on sympathy strikes).

When Is a Union Prohibited from Striking?

- Wildcat strikes. We have already discussed wildcat strikes in Chapter 5. As you may recall, these are strikes that are not authorized by the union.

- Sympathy strikes, if specifically banned by the collective bargaining agreement.
- When a contract containing a no-strike clause is in effect.
- During the term of a valid contract extension.
- Striking without giving sufficient notice pursuant to the terms of a strike notification agreement.
- In the case where there has been a collective agreement in existence, striking without having given appropriate notice to the Federal Mediation and Conciliation Service (FMCS) as required in Section 8 of the Act. The relevant portion of this section is as follows:

[t]he duty to bargain collectively shall also mean that no party to such contract shall terminate or modify such contract, unless the party desiring such termination or modification—

(1) serves a written notice upon the other party to the contract of the proposed termination or modification sixty days prior to the expiration date thereof, or in the event such contract contains no expiration date, sixty days prior to the time it is proposed to make such termination or modification;

(2) offers to meet and confer with the other party for the purpose of negotiating a new contract or a contract containing the proposed modifications;

(3) notifies the Federal Mediation and Conciliation Service within thirty days after such notice of the existence of a dispute, and simultaneously therewith notifies any State or Territorial agency established to mediate and conciliate disputes within the State or Territory where the dispute occurred, provided no agreement has been reached by that time; and

(4) continues in full force and effect, without resorting to strike or lockout, all the terms and conditions of the existing contract for a period of sixty days after such notice is given or until the expiration date of such contract, whichever occurs later:

The duties imposed upon employers, employees, and labor organizations by paragraphs (2), (3), and (4) [paragraphs (2) to (4) of this subsection] shall become inapplicable upon an intervening certification of the Board, under which the labor organization or individual, which is a party to the contract, has been superseded as or ceased to be the representative of the employees subject to the provisions of section 9(a) [section 159(a) of this title], and the duties so imposed shall not be construed as requiring either party to discuss or agree to any modification of the terms and conditions contained in a contract for a fixed period, if such modification is to become effective before such terms and conditions can be reopened under the provisions of the contract. Any employee who engages in a strike within any notice period specified in this subsection, or who engages in any strike within the appropriate period specified in subsection (g) of this section, shall lose his status as an employee of the employer engaged in the particular labor dispute, for the purposes of sections 8, 9, and 10 of this Act [sections 158, 159, and 160 of this title], but such loss of status for such employee shall terminate if and when he is re-employed by such employer. Whenever the collective bargaining involves employees of a healthcare institution, the provisions of this section 8(d) [this subsection] shall be modified as follows:

(A) The notice of section 8(d)(1) [paragraph (1) of this subsection] shall be ninety days; the notice of section 8(d)(3) [paragraph (3) of this subsection] shall be sixty days; and the contract period of section 8(d)(4) [paragraph (4) of this subsection] shall be ninety days.

(B) Where the bargaining is for an initial agreement following certification or recognition, at least thirty days' notice of the existence of a dispute shall be given by the labor organization to the agencies set forth in section 8(d)(3) [in paragraph (3) of this subsection].

(C) After notice is given to the Federal Mediation and Conciliation Service under either clause (A) or (B) of this sentence, the Service shall promptly communicate with the parties and use its best efforts, by mediation and conciliation, to bring them to agreement. The parties shall participate fully and promptly in such meetings as may be undertaken by the Service for the purpose of aiding in a settlement of the dispute.

Economic and Unfair Labor Practice Strikes

Economic and unfair labor practices are the two most common forms of strikes.

An economic strike is one that is caused by the union's dissatisfaction over the terms and conditions of employment offered during bargaining. As noted elsewhere, the union does not have to wait for an impasse to occur before going out on strike. (Obviously, it must await contract expiration.) The bargaining obligation, moreover, remains until an impasse or agreement is reached.

If employees go out on an economic strike, they can be replaced, either temporarily or permanently, at the option of the employer. Under this rule, the employer who permanently replaces a striking worker can refuse to take this person back even though the person has offered to come back to work. This is a rather controversial part of the law, but it has remained unchanged since the U.S. Supreme Court first declared this right of the employer in a case involving Mackay Radio & Telegraph Co. decided in 1938.*

---

* NLRB v. Mackay Radio & Telegraph Co., 304 U.S. 333 (1938).

Under Board precedent decided in the 1968 case of Laidlaw Corp.,* such replaced employees are not entitled to reinstatement until the departure of the replacement, i.e., a vacancy that the employee is qualified to fill. In essence, this means that the permanently replaced strikers are placed on a preferential hire list. When a vacancy comes open for which they are qualified, they must be rehired if they unconditionally have offered to return to work. If, on the other hand, the employee has found regular employment elsewhere in a substantially equivalent position, there is no obligation to fill the vacancy with the former striker.

Combined with the fact that economic strikers are ineligible for unemployment compensation in most states, there is a definite disincentive to strike.

On the other hand, an unfair labor practice strike is one that has been precipitated or prolonged by the employer's unfair labor practices. In the case of an unfair labor practice strike, strikers are entitled to reinstatement upon making an unconditional offer to return to work, even if replacements have been hired. In other words, such employees may be replaced only temporarily. If they are not reinstated upon making such an offer, the employer will be liable for back pay and, at the conclusion of the unfair labor practice proceedings, they will be reinstated.

As you may see, it is in the union's best interest to characterize a strike as an unfair labor practice strike. This puts some pressure on the employer because, even if the company does not believe it has committed any unfair labor practices, it will not know for sure until the end of the unfair labor practice proceedings or until the union drops the charge (usually in exchange for contract concessions and reinstatement of all strikers who want to come back to work).

To complicate the scenario, a strike that started out as an economic strike may be converted to an unfair labor practice strike after its commencement. Any strike replacements hired before the date of conversion will be permanent. Replacements hired thereafter may be temporary only.

The determination as to whether a strike is an unfair labor practice strike is ultimately up to the Board. Two basic elements must be shown:

1. That the employer, in fact, has committed an unfair labor practice.
2. That the unlawful employer action either caused or prolonged the strike.

It is important to note that the unfair labor practice need not be the sole cause of the strike in order for the strike to be of the unfair labor practice variety. On the other hand, there must be an established unfair labor practice. Just because the union or employees mistakenly believe an employer has committed an unfair labor practice, this will not make the strike an unfair labor practice strike.

---

* Laidlaw Corp., 171 NLRB 1366 (1968).

The Board will mainly look to the type of unfair labor practice committed, the number or magnitude of the unfair practices, and employees' knowledge of and reaction to the unfair labor practices.

The Board also will examine the relationship between the unfair labor practice and the parties' failure to reach an agreement during bargaining. Clearly, if the unfair labor practice is of the "failure-to-bargain-in-good-faith" variety, it may be held to have caused the failure and, therefore, the strike.

The issue of whether the strike is economic or an unfair labor practice strike often puts the employer in a difficult position with replacement workers. Usually, it is best to tell these employees what the situation is and whether they will be able to keep their jobs, which may depend on the outcome of the unfair labor practice proceedings.

In most states, employers have to advise applicants for employment if a labor dispute is in progress.

Unprotected Activities during an Otherwise Lawful Strike

Trespass

As a general rule, strikers are not allowed to trespass on private property in order to picket or distribute handbills. There may be exceptions to this rule depending on the layout of the facility and whether access is necessary in order to be able to picket or handbill.

This can become a tricky issue in the case of shopping malls or similar facilities. The Board has ruled that under some circumstances the rights of the private property owner are outweighed by the interest of the union in picketing.

Some of the factors the Board considers include:

- Manner in which the picketing is carried out (picketing that becomes violent loses its protection)
- The relationship of the employer to the property involved (i.e., owner, lessee, tenant, etc.)
- Who is the union trying to "reach" with the picketing (i.e., employees of the struck employer or someone else)
- The danger of involving neutral employers in the picketing
- How practical are the union's alternatives to communicate its message if access to the private property is denied
- Safety issues if the union is forced to picket on public property, such as roadways
- The property's size and openness
- The use to which the property is put

The Board has gone to great lengths to protect the union's right to picket. In one case, it allowed employees to picket in the elevator lobby on the fourteenth floor of a high-rise building because the union had no other way to reach its audience. The facts in this case were somewhat unusual. For instance, the building was accessed by many skywalks and tunnels, making picketing in front of the building (the traditional method) ineffective.

Thus, never assume you can "kick the union off" private property. Many times you *will* be able to do this, but the company should consult with legal counsel first.

Naturally, you must know where the boundaries to the property are. A mistake in this respect could be embarrassing and costly.

If you have determined that the strikers have no right to be on your property, ask them to leave and warn them you will call law enforcement if they remain. Call law enforcement only if they refuse.

Violence

Nothing in the National Labor Relations Act gives striking employees the right to engage in violent acts. Such acts often constitute violations of state criminal law as well as lead to unfair labor practice charges against the union. Strikers who engage in picket line violence may often be discharged. Those who assist, authorize, or encourage such activities also may lose protection under the law.

Unfortunately, violence and strikes often go hand in hand. Emotions are high as are the stakes. Violence is especially likely if the employer hires striker replacements.

Employers often respond to such activities with requests to the local state court to issue an injunction to stop the violence. If such an order is issued, and the violence continues, those responsible may be found guilty of contempt of court. Employers often persuade local prosecutors to bring criminal charges against strikers who engage in violent activities.

Blocking Entry and Exit

The union is not allowed to physically prevent people and vehicles from entering or exiting the employer's premises. If this occurs, many employers will seek police assistance and/or an injunction. Such activity also may constitute an unfair labor practice and/or grounds for discharge of the offending employee–strikers. The Board, however, will take into consideration how long the blocking took place. A few seconds or minutes may not be enough to make the blocking unlawful insofar as unfair labor practice charges are concerned.

Current law holds that verbal threats, intimidating conduct, and name calling could constitute an unfair labor practice and/or cause the employee to lose protection if these activities would reasonably tend to coerce or intimidate the target employees (i.e., those crossing the picket line) in the exercise of their right under Section 7 to refrain from union activity. Usually, however, calling strikebreakers profane or vulgar names will not constitute a violation. It is the threat of physical harm that usually must be present to remove legal protections from the strikers.

Damage to Property.

Unfortunately, many times strikers get carried away and do such things as throw bricks, scatter glass or nails, sabotage equipment, even turn over buses bringing replacement workers. These activities also are unprotected both under the NLRA and state law.

Investigation of Picket Line Misconduct

As a supervisor, you might be asked to gather evidence to support an injunction, an unfair labor practice against the union, or termination of a striker for misconduct. Investigation of such events is similar to that undertaken for other disciplinary actions.

If the company is seeking injunctive relief, you may be asked to sign an affidavit or even testify in a court proceeding where the judge will determine if an injunction should be issued.

One important thing to be aware of when determining discipline for picket line misconduct is that you must not enforce the rules selectively. In other words, if you discharge one striker, but do nothing to another who engaged in the same misconduct, you may find yourself charged with an unfair labor practice. This would be especially so if you terminated a striker for a physical assault, but did not terminate a replacement employee who committed a similar offense.

In-Plant Work Stoppages

In many instances, these types of activities, such as the old sit-down strike, are illegal and employees have no protection from discharge.

There are a few instances, however, when an in-plant work stoppage will be protected. A recent Board case involving Quietflex Manufacturing Company illustrates this point.*

In this case, about eighty employees of Hispanic origin stopped work in protest of their pay and working conditions (they thought non-Hispanic employees were being treated better). They gathered in the parking lot where they presented a list of demands to the employer. After this, they were ordered back to work, but refused. At that point, the company told them they must leave, but they refused. The company told them a second time to leave, but they did not until the sheriff showed up at the plant.

All in all, the work stoppage lasted twelve hours.

---

* Quietflex Manufacturing Co., 3444 NLRB 1055 (2005).

The Board, citing earlier precedent, set forth the factors that should be considered when determining if the in-plant work stoppage is protected activity. These factors include:

- What is the reason why the employees have stopped working?
- Did the employees engage in violent conduct or was it peaceful?
- Did the stoppage interfere with production?
- Did the stoppage deprive the employer of access to its facility?
- Did the employees have an adequate opportunity to present their grievances that led to the stoppage?
- Did the employer warn the employees that they must leave or face termination of employment?
- Did the employees remain on the premises after their shift ended?
- How long did the stoppage last?
- Were the employees represented by a labor organization?
- Did the employees attempt to seize employer property or damage it?

In this case, the Board held the activity was unprotected mainly because the stoppage lasted twelve hours and continued after the employees presented their demands to the employer.

Intermittent Strikes

Some unions are tempted to engage in a series of "quickie" strikes, where members strike for a short period of time and offer to return to work before the employer can replace them. Additionally, if allowed to take place, such strikes would not result in the loss of wages to the same extent as a more traditional strike.

Most intermittent strikes are unlawful. If, however, a series of strikes were due to entirely different causes, the strikes might be ruled protected.

Statements by Strikers That Disparage the Employer's Product or Service

Even though they are on strike, strikers are still employees and can be held to some basic standards of loyalty to the employer. In 1951, the U.S. Supreme Court held that remarks that disparage the employer's product, rather than publicize a labor dispute, are unprotected. To be protected, the remarks must somehow relate to the labor dispute or to terms and conditions of employment. Strikers who think they can "slam" their employer by denigrating what it produces may be in for a surprise.

Secondary Boycotts

As noted earlier in this book, the law generally prohibits a union from bringing pressure on neutral third parties in hopes that they will, in turn, put pressure on the employer with whom they have a dispute to give in to the union's demands. The employer with whom the employees have the dispute is usually referred to as the "primary employer." For instance, the union could not put up a picket line around one of the primary employer's best customers in order for the customer to put pressure on the primary employer.

The distinction between the primary employer and a supposed neutral employer is not always that clear. For instance, if the primary employer, unable to supply its customers due to a strike at its facility, sent work to another employer, the union could picket that employer as well as the primary. This is known as the "ally doctrine" and is well established in labor law.

The situation might be different, however, if the customers directly approached the third company because they could not get deliveries from the primary. In this case, the union probably could not picket the neutral employer unless it could be shown that the primary employer had some hand in arranging for other companies to do its work or if the primary employer was the one actually paying for the work, instead of the customer.

Sometimes, the relationship between two companies is so close that the law views them as one company for purposes of determining issues arising in the secondary boycott scenario. Generally speaking, if two companies share common ownership, common management, have interrelated operations, and centralized control of labor relations, the Board probably will view them as one company, and the union, therefore, may picket both companies.

Ambulatory Picketing

While neutrals are generally protected from picketing, what happens when the primary employer is temporarily on the property of a neutral employer? Let us say that the employees of a trucking company are on strike. Where can they picket? Clearly, they could picket at the company's headquarters. But, what about the company's trucks that go from place to place making deliveries?

With some restrictions, the law generally allows unions to engage in ambulatory picketing, sometimes referred to as *picketing between the headlights*. In other words, the law considers the truck of the primary employer also to be a **site of the dispute**, just as much as the company offices.

This law was established in a case involving the Moore Dry Dock Company back in 1950 and it actually involved a ship, not trucks.* The ship belonged to another company, not Moore Dry Dock, but was in the dry dock for repairs. The union of seamen had a dispute with the owner of the ship and the union picketed the ship while it was at Moore Dry Dock. Moore employees ceased working on the ship in question. Naturally, Moore was unhappy and filed a charge with the Board.

---

* Sailors Union of the Pacific, 92 NLRB 547 (1950).

The Board held that the picketing was primary in nature because of the following circumstances:

- The picketing was confined to the time when the primary employer's vessel was on the premises of Moore.
- The primary employer was engaged in its normal business on the site (here getting its boat fixed).
- The picketing was located reasonably close to the vessel (i.e., not all over Moore's property).
- The picket signs and other written materials clearly disclosed that the dispute was with the owner of the ship, not Moore.

This may be easily applied to our truck example mentioned above. If the union pickets only when the trucks are there; the trucks are making deliveries, which is a normal part of the business of the primary employer; the pickets stay as close to the trucks as they can; and their signs clearly note that their dispute is with the trucking company, their action should be held lawful.

Common Situs Picketing

Construction Situation

Related to the ambulatory issue is the situation where there are several neutral employers working on a job site along with an employer who has a labor dispute with the union representing his employees. This is a common situation in the construction industry. Because the primary employer is at the construction site, then this is considered a site of the dispute and the union may picket.

Naturally, such a picket outside the gate of a construction site could have a dramatic impact on the entire project. Many of the employees of the neutral employers may refuse to cross the union's picket line.

In order to avoid what otherwise might be a shut down of the site, the practice of establishing a **reserved gate** has developed. This entails creating a separate gate for the employees of the primary employer as well as its suppliers and vendors. Employees of all the neutral companies (and the suppliers and vendors of those companies) must use another gate. Usually, someone representing the neutral employers or perhaps the struck employer will notify the union in writing of the existence of the reserve gate and request that the union confine its picketing to that gate. If the union refuses, a secondary boycott charge may be filed with the Board and the union may be liable for damages.

There are two things to consider here. There must be adequate signage at the gates informing employees, suppliers, and vendors which gate they are supposed to use. Usually, these signs are placed so they are visible to those both entering and exiting the property.

Second, if the gates are not used in accordance with the instruction, the reserve gate system is "tainted" and the union may be able to picket at any gate. Thus, someone should monitor the gates and ensure they are used properly in accordance with the posted signs.

The General Electric Scenario

What happens if, instead of the primary employer being on the premises of a neutral employer (like Moore Dry Dock), the reverse is true—the neutral is on the premises of the primary employer.

This was the situation in a case involving the General Electric Company in 1961.* This case found its way to the U.S. Supreme Court. One of the bargaining units at GE was on strike. There were several gates at the plant. The union set up pickets outside all of the gates including one that was reserved for independent contractors performing work on GE property. This was so despite the fact that there was a sign indicating the gate in question was to be used only employees of contractors and that GE employees were supposed to use other gates.

The Supreme Court held that in this situation, the normal reserved gate rules are not applicable, ostensibly because the primary employer owns the site. The Court drew a distinction based on what type of work the contractor was doing. If the contractor was doing work for the primary employer necessary to sustain its normal operations, then the union could picket the gate used by that contractor. Similarly, if the employer is taking advantage of the shut down caused by the strike to do projects that could otherwise not have been done during normal operations, then the union could picket the gates used by these contractors as well. The idea here is that contractors performing this kind of work are more allied to the employer and less neutral and, therefore, may not be protected from those picketing as they enter and leave the primary employer's premises.

On the other hand, if the contractor is performing work unrelated to normal operations and/or if the work could be done without curtailing normal operations, then the contractor is considered a neutral. For example, if the contractor was erecting a new building that, if done during normal operations, would not have required a curtailment of those operations, then they would be protected from picketing (assuming they used a separate gate).

Special Rules for Strikes at Healthcare Establishments

A work stoppage at a hospital or nursing home is obviously a sensitive matter due to the possible impact on the health of patients or residents. Because of this, in 1974, Congress passed a law, the gist of which requires a union to give more

---

* Local 761, International Union of Electrical, Radio & Machine Workers v. NLRB, 366 U.S. 667 (1961).

notice of a labor dispute or strike as compared with the rules for nonhealthcare employers.

A "healthcare institution" is defined by the law to include:

- Hospital or convalescent hospital
- Health maintenance organization
- Health clinic
- Nursing home
- Extended care facility
- Other institutions "devoted to the care of sick, infirm, or aged persons"

As you may recall, section 8(d) of the NLRA requires that a party, desiring to amend/terminate/modify a labor agreement, gives the other party and the FMCS sixty days written notice of such intent. If they do not, then they cannot exercise their economic weapons (strike or lockout) until such notice has been given. This is often referred to as a "cooling off period." Basically, the 1974 laws extends this to ninety days for healthcare institutions.

Finally, the law requires a union intending to strike or picket to give a healthcare institution at least a ten-day notice of its intent to engage in such activity.

The law has been interpreted to mean that a union cannot unilaterally extend the notice period. In other words, it cannot give the ten-day notice, let the ten days pass, and then surprise the employer with a strike at some later time. This would defeat the purpose of the notice period. Of course, the parties may extend the notice by mutual agreement.

Employees who strike when the proper notice has not been given are not protected from discharge.

Lockouts

A lockout is a temporary cessation of business by the employer who tells its employees that they will not be allowed to work until a contract with the union is reached. **Thus, a lockout can be viewed as a work stoppage caused by the employer at a time of its choosing.**

The first thing to note about a lockout is that it cannot occur while there is an existing contract with a no-lockout clause in it. This rule is similar to the one wherein a no-strike clause of an existing agreement bars a strike during its term.

A second point is that, as in the case of a union that wishes to strike, the employer must have given appropriate notice under Section 8(d) in order to be able to engage in a lockout.

However, the above two restrictions are not the only ones.

The Board and the courts have held that an employer must have bargained in good faith before instituting a lockout. Over the years, there has been some dispute as to whether an employer and union had to be at impasse before the employer may initiate a lockout.

In 1964, the U.S. Supreme Court decided a case involving the American Ship Building Company.* There is language in this opinion that would indicate that the parties must be at impasse before an employer can resort to lockout. On the other hand, the Board held in a 1968 decision involving Darling & Company† that reaching an impasse may not be a prerequisite to lock out employees so long as the employer had bargained in good faith up to the point of lockout.

In my opinion, an employer should consider lockout only if the parties are at impasse. The stakes are too high to risk an unfair labor practice charge being successful. If you unlawfully lock out employees, you may be liable for the wages they would have earned had you not locked them out.

There is one exception to my opinion. That is when the timing of a work stoppage is crucial to an employer's business. For instance, this would apply to a business that was seasonal. The union will want to strike at the height of the season in order to bring maximum pressure to bear on the employer. An employer, not wanting to be in this situation, may prefer to have the work stoppage occur prior to the "high season." An employer in this situation may want to resort to a lockout, even if the parties are not at an impasse. This is seen especially where the employer's product is perishable.

Another time when a lockout is usually lawful is when a union strikes one member of a multiemployer bargaining unit, but keeps working at the other employers in order to try to drive a wedge in the group (this is sometimes called a "whipsaw strike"). The law has allowed all of the employers to lock out in this situation to maintain solidarity and thwart the union's attempt to weaken the bargaining group.

In all of this, we are assuming that the lockout is in support of the employer's bargaining position. If the employer locks out to punish the employees or in order to destroy the union, it may be found to be a violation of the law.

The law also allows an employer to hire **temporary** replacements for the locked out employees. This assumes, of course, that the lockout itself is lawful.

In most states, employees who are locked out will be eligible for unemployment compensation.

The lockout is a drastic weapon, and fraught with many opportunities for the employer to make expensive mistakes, especially if it replaces employees. A lockout should never be undertaken without careful consideration of its benefits versus the disadvantages, which are substantial, not only from a legal point of view, but also from a labor relations perspective.

---

* American Shipbuilding Company v. NLRB, 379 U.S. 814 (1964).
† Darling & Company, 170 NLRB No. 127 (1968).

Appendix 1

Right to Work States

Alabama

Arizona

Arkansas

Florida

Georgia

Idaho

Iowa

Kansas

Louisiana

Mississippi

Nebraska

Nevada

North Carolina

North Dakota

Oklahoma

South Carolina

South Dakota

Tennessee

Texas

Utah

Virginia

Wyoming

Appendix 2

Web Sites of Labor and Employment Law Sources

AFL-CIO: www.aflcio.org

AMERICAN BAR ASSOCIATION: www.abanet.org

BNA: www.bna.com

BUREAU OF LABOR STATISTICS: stats.bls.gov

CHAMBER OF COMMERCE: www.uschamber.org

CODE OF FEDERAL REGULATIONS: http://www.gpoaccess.gov/cfr/index.html

CONGRESSIONAL RECORD: www.access.gpo.gov/sudocs/aces/aces150html

DAILY LABOR REPORT: www.bna.com/newsstand

DEPARTMENT OF JUSTICE: www.usdoj.gov

DEPARTMENT OF LABOR: www.dol.gov

EEOC: www.eeoc.gov

FIND LAW: www.findlaw.com

HOUSE OF REPRESENTATIVES: www.house.gov

NATIONAL ASSOCIATION OF MANUFACTURERS: www.nam.org

NATIONAL LABOR RELATIONS BOARD: www.nlrb.gov

OKLAHOMA SUPREME COURT: www.oscn.net

OSHA: www.osha.gov

U.S. CODE: http://www4.law.cornell.edu/uscode

U.S. SENATE: www.senate.gov

WHITE HOUSE: www.whitehouse.gov

SHRM: www.shrm.org/government

CHANGE TO WIN FEDERATION: www.changetowin.org

Appendix 3

Sample Management Rights Clause

The Company retains the exclusive right to manage the business. All the rights, powers, functions, and authority of the Company that it had prior to the time any Union became certified as exclusive bargaining representative of employees of the Company and that are not explicitly abridged by a specific provision of this Agreement, are retained by the Company. Among the rights that the Company specifically retains are the rights to establish rules of conduct; to plan, direct, and control operations; to schedule and assign work to employees; to determine the means, methods, processes, and schedules of operation; subcontract or contract out all or any part of the work that may be performed either more economically or expeditiously or for any other reason deemed sufficient by the Company; to establish standards and to maintain the standards and to maintain the efficiency of employees; to establish and require employees to observe Company rules and regulations; to hire, lay off, or relieve employees from duties for lack of work or other legitimate reasons; and to maintain order and to suspend, promote, demote, discipline, and discharge employees for just cause. The Company also retains the right to close all or a portion of the facilities covered by this Agreement or to sell, relocate, or in any other way to dispose of or convert such facilities.

The exercise of any right enumerated in this Article herein shall not be considered or construed as a violation of the Agreement, or in violation of any rights possessed by the Union or by bargaining unit employees.

Appendix 4

Sample No Strikes/No Lockouts Clause

Section 1   There shall be no strike, sympathy strike, concerted refusal to report for work, slowdown, stoppage of work, planned inefficiency, sick out, sit down, or any other interruption of work or production (or threat or inducement of the same) by the Union or any employee during the term of this Agreement. The Company agrees not to lock out any employee covered by this Agreement during the term thereof. A layoff of employees for economic or other legitimate business reasons does not constitute a lockout.

Section 2   The Union agrees that neither it nor any of the employees in the bargaining unit covered by this Agreement will collectively, concertedly, or individually engage in or participate, directly or indirectly, in any of the activity prohibited by this Article.

Section 3   Furthermore, it is understood that no union officer, representative, or agent may authorize, encourage, or assist in any strike, sympathy strike, concerted refusal to report for work, slowdown, stoppage of work, planned inefficiency, sick out, sit down, or any other interruption of work on any premises of the Company, nor will the Union, its officers, representatives, or agents participate in, counsel, or induce any such activity. This clause also specifically prohibits any employee from refusing to report for work or refusing to work due to the existence of a picket line.

Section 4   The Union, its officers, agents, members, and employees covered by this Agreement, agree that they will take all affirmative action legally available to prevent any activity prohibited by this Article.

Section 5   In the event of activity prohibited by this Article, the Union will do the following:

(a) Notify all employees immediately (both orally and in writing) that the interruption of work is unauthorized and in violation of the Agreement, and that they should immediately return to work.

(b) Make every other reasonable effort to have employees cease and desist from violation of this Article.

Section 6   It is further understood that any employee who threatens, participates in, or encourages a violation of this Article shall, in the sole discretion of the Company, be subject to immediate discharge.

Appendix 5

Sample Zipper Clause

This Agreement is subject to amendment, alteration, or addition only by a subsequent written agreement between and executed by authorized representatives of the Company and the Union. The waiver of any breach, term, or condition of this Agreement by either party shall not constitute a precedent in the future enforcement of all these terms and conditions. The parties acknowledge that during negotiations that resulted in this Agreement, each had the unlimited right and opportunity to make demands and proposals with respect to any subject or matter not removed by law from the area of collective bargaining, and that the understandings and agreements arrived at by the parties after the exercise of that right and opportunity are set forth in this Agreement. The parties acknowledge that this Agreement contains the full and complete Agreement on all subjects upon which the parties did bargain or could have bargained. All matters not included in this Agreement shall be deemed to have been raised and disposed of as if covered herein. Therefore, the Company and the Union, for the life of this Agreement, each voluntarily and unqualifiedly waives the right and each agrees that the other shall not be obligated to bargain collectively with respect to any subject or matter referred to, or covered in this Agreement, or with respect to any matter or subject not specifically referred to or covered in this Agreement, or with respect to any provision voided by law, even though such subjects or matters may not have been within the knowledge or contemplation of either or both of the parties at the time that they negotiated or signed this Agreement. Except to the extent specifically limited in this Article, nothing herein shall relieve the Company from its obligation under the Act with regard to unilateral changes of mandatory subjects of bargaining.

Appendix 6

Sample Union Authorization Card

AUTHORIZATION FOR REPRESENTATION

I authorize a local union of the International Brotherhood of Electrical Workers, to represent me in collective bargaining with my employer.

Name..
(Please Print)

Address...Phone.......................

City...State ....Zip ....

S.S. # ....

Employer ....

Department ....Shift: 1st ❑   2nd ❑   3rd

Job Classification ....

Date .... Signature ....

Form 141

Appendix 7

Solicitation

Can the Employer Ban Solicitation by Employees?	Working Areas	Nonworking Areas
Working Time	Yes	Yes
Nonworking Time	No	No

Appendix 8

Distribution of Literature

Can the Employer Ban the Distribution of Literature by Employees?	Working Areas	Nonworking Areas
Working Time	Yes	Yes
Nonworking Time	Yes	No

Appendix 9

Sample NLRB Petition

INTERNET FORM NLRB-502 (2-08)	UNITED STATES GOVERNMENT NATIONAL LABOR RELATIONS BOARD **PETITION**	FORM EXEMPT UNDER 44 U.S.C. DO NOT WRITE IN THIS SPACE
		Case No. Date Filed

INSTRUCTIONS: Submit an original of this Petition to the NLRB Regional Office in the Region in which the employer concerned is located.

The Petitioner alleges that the following circumstances exist and requests that the NLRB proceed under its proper authority pursuant to Section 9 of the NLRA.

1. PURPOSE OF THIS PETITION (if box RC, RM, or RD is checked and a charge under Section 8(b)(7) of the Act has been filed involving the Employer named herein, the statement following the description of the type of petition shall not be deemed made.) (Check One)

☐ **RC-CERTIFICATION OF REPRESENTATIVE** - A substantial number of employees wish to be represented for purposes of collective bargaining by Petitioner and Petitioner desires to be certified as representative of the employees.

☐ **RM-REPRESENTATION (EMPLOYER PETITION)** - One or more individuals or labor organizations have presented a claim to Petitioner to be recognized as the representative of employees of Petitioner.

☐ **RD-DECERTIFICATION (REMOVAL OF REPRESENTATIVE)** - A substantial number of employees assert that the certified or currently recognized bargaining representative is no longer their representative.

☐ **UD-WITHDRAWAL OF UNION SHOP AUTHORITY (REMOVAL OF OBLIGATION TO PAY DUES)** - Thirty percent (30%) or more of employees in a bargaining unit covered by an agreement between their employer and a labor organization desire that such authority be rescinded.

☐ **UC-UNIT CLARIFICATION-** A labor organization is currently recognized by Employer, but Petitioner seeks clarification of placement of certain employees (Check one) ☐ In unit previously certified. ☐ In unit not previously certified in Case No. _____

☐ **AC-AMENDMENT OF CERTIFICATION-** Petitioner seeks amendment of certification issued in Case No. _____ Attach statement describing the specific amendment sought.

2. Name of Employer	Employer Representative to contact	Tel. No.

3. Address(es) of Establishment(s) involved (Street and number, city, State, ZIP code)	Fax No.

4a. Type of Establishment (Factory, mine, wholesaler, etc.)	4b. Identify principal product or service	Cell No. / e-Mail

5. Unit Involved (In UC petition, describe **present** bargaining unit and attach description of proposed clarification.)	6a. Number of Employees in Unit:
Included	Present
Excluded	Proposed (By UC/AC)
	6b. Is this petition supported by 30% or more of the employees in the unit?* ☐ Yes ☐ No *Not applicable in RM, UC, and AC

(If you have checked box RC in 1 above, check and complete EITHER item 7a or 7b, whichever is applicable)

7a. ☐ Request for recognition as Bargaining Representative was made on (Date) _____ and Employer declined recognition on or about (Date) _____ (If no reply received, so state).

7b. ☐ Petitioner is currently recognized as Bargaining Representative and desires certification under the Act.

8. Name of Recognized or Certified Bargaining Agent (If none, so state.)	Affiliation
Address	Tel. No. / Cell No.	Date of Recognition or Certification / Fax No. / e-Mail

9. Expiration Date of Current Contract, If any (Month, Day, Year)	10. If you have checked box UD in 1 above, show here the date of execution of agreement granting union shop (Month, Day and Year)

11a. Is there now a strike or picketing at the Employer's establishment(s) Involved? Yes ☐ No ☐	11b. If so, approximately how many employees are participating?

11c. The Employer has been picketed by or on behalf of (Insert Name) _____, a labor organization, of (Insert Address) _____ Since (Month, Day, Year) _____

12. Organizations or individuals other than Petitioner (and other than those named in items 8 and 11c), which have claimed recognition as representatives and other organizations and individuals known to have a representative interest in any employees in unit described in item 5 above. (If none, so state)

Name	Address	Tel. No. / Cell No.	Fax No. / e-Mail

13. Full name of party filing petition (If labor organization, give full name, including local name and number)

14a. Address (street and number, city, state, and ZIP code)	14b. Tel. No. EXT / 14d. Cell No.	14c. Fax No. / 14e. e-Mail

15. Full name of national or international labor organization of which Petitioner is an affiliate or constituent (to be filled in when petition is filed by a labor organization)

I declare that I have read the above petition and that the statements are true to the best of my knowledge and belief.

Name (Print)	Signature	Title (if any)
Address (street and number, city, state, and ZIP code)	Tel. No. / Cell No.	Fax No. / eMail

WILLFUL FALSE STATEMENTS ON THIS PETITION CAN BE PUNISHED BY FINE AND IMPRISONMENT (U.S. CODE, TITLE 18, SECTION 1001)

PRIVACY ACT STATEMENT

Solicitation of the information on this form is authorized by the National Labor Relations Act (NLRA), 29 U.S.C. § 151 et seq. The principal use of the information is to assist the National Labor Relations Board (NLRB) in processing unfair labor practice and related proceedings or litigation. The routine uses for the information are fully set forth in the Federal Register, 71 Fed. Reg. 74942-43 (Dec. 13, 2006). The NLRB will further explain these uses upon request. Disclosure of this information to the NLRB is voluntary; however, failure to supply the information will cause the NLRB to decline to invoke its processes.

Appendix 10

Sample Unfair Labor Practice Charge

FORM EXEMPT UNDER 44 U.S.C 3512

INTERNET FORM NLRB-501 (2-08)	UNITED STATES OF AMERICA NATIONAL LABOR RELATIONS BOARD CHARGE AGAINST EMPLOYER	DO NOT WRITE IN THIS SPACE	
		Case	Date Filed

INSTRUCTIONS:
File an original with NLRB Regional Director for the region in which the alleged unfair labor practice occurred or is occurring.

1. EMPLOYER AGAINST WHOM CHARGE IS BROUGHT

a. Name of Employer		b. Tel. No.
		c. Cell No.
		f. Fax No.
d. Address *(Street, city, state, and ZIP code)*	e. Employer Representative	g. e-Mail
		h. Number of workers employed
i. Type of Establishment *(factory, mine, wholesaler, etc.)*	j. Identify principal product or service	

k. The above-named employer has engaged in and is engaging in unfair labor practices within the meaning of section 8(a), subsections (1) and *(list subsections)* of the National Labor Relations Act, and these unfair labor practices are practices affecting commerce within the meaning of the Act, or these unfair labor practices are unfair practices affecting commerce within the meaning of the Act and the Postal Reorganization Act.

2. Basis of the Charge *(set forth a clear and concise statement of the facts constituting the alleged unfair labor practices)*

3. Full name of party filing charge *(if labor organization, give full name, including local name and number)*

4a. Address *(Street and number, city, state, and ZIP code)*	4b. Tel. No.
	4c. Cell No.
	4d. Fax No.
	4e. e-Mail

5. Full name of national or international labor organization of which it is an affiliate or constituent unit *(to be filled in when charge is filed by a labor organization)*

6. DECLARATION I declare that I have read the above charge and that the statements are true to the best of my knowledge and belief.	Tel. No.
	Office, if any, Cell No.
By _____ _____ (signature of representative or person making charge) (Print/type name and title or office, if any)	Fax No.
	e-Mail
Address _____ (date)	

WILLFUL FALSE STATEMENTS ON THIS CHARGE CAN BE PUNISHED BY FINE AND IMPRISONMENT (U.S. CODE, TITLE 18, SECTION 1001)
PRIVACY ACT STATEMENT

Solicitation of the information on this form is authorized by the National Labor Relations Act (NLRA), 29 U.S.C. § 151 *et seq.* The principal use of the information is to assist the National Labor Relations Board (NLRB) in processing unfair labor practice and related proceedings or litigation. The routine uses for the information are fully set forth in the Federal Register, 71 Fed. Reg. 74942-43 (Dec. 13, 2006). The NLRB will further explain these uses upon request. Disclosure of this information to the NLRB is voluntary; however, failure to supply the information will cause the NLRB to decline to invoke its processes.

Appendix 11

Tips for Witnesses in Arbitration Proceedings

So, you're going to be a witness in an arbitration? Try not to worry and calm down. It's not as bad as you think. Here are a few pointers that may help. Read them over now and then again just before you go into the arbitration hearing. If you have any questions, ask your supervisor or the company representative.

- **Tell the truth.** You will be sworn to tell the truth by the arbitrator or a court reporter. This is your most important job. Make sure you also tell the truth to the person calling you as a witness—the whole truth—so that there will be no surprises. Remember, no case is so important that you should lie or stretch the truth to try to win.
- **Answer the question asked, then quit.** You are not on the witness stand to tell a story or make a speech. You are there to answer questions. This instruction can be broken down into three parts:

  Listen very carefully to the question

  Answer THE QUESTION ASKED

  Stop talking until asked the next question

- **If you don't understand a question, tell the person asking you.** Have him or her rephrase it, repeat it ... whatever it takes. You must understand the question in order to answer it truthfully.
- **If you don't know the answer to the question, say so.** Don't guess or speculate. In normal conversation, I might ask you who will win the Super Bowl this year. Almost everyone has an opinion, but the truth of the matter is, they don't know. In an arbitration hearing, only answer the question if you *know* the answer.
- **If you don't remember, say so.** If I asked you who won the World Series in 1985, you might guess even though you really don't know. We all do this in

normal conversation, but you shouldn't do it in an arbitration hearing. If you don't remember, say so.

Be courteous and direct in your answers. Nobody likes (or trusts) a witness who is combative or acts like he or she has something to hide.

Don't patronize or demean the questioner or the arbitrator. You may be the smartest person in the room, but there is no reason to speak down to others. Treat everyone in the room as your intellectual equal.

You have to be thinking clearly. There is no time to let your mind wander when you are testifying. You have to be fully alert and at your mental best.

Let the questioner finish asking the question before you start giving your answer. Avoid talking at the same time as someone else. It is confusing and frustrating for the arbitrator.

Avoid shakes and nods of the head and "uh huhs," etc. Answer all questions out loud. This is especially important if there is a court reporter present.

Avoid putting your hands over your mouth when answering questions. The reason for this rule should be obvious.

When giving your answers, look directly at the questioner, especially if it is the arbitrator asking you questions.

Think about each question before answering. Remember, you are under oath. You have the absolute right to think about the question and your answer. Just don't carry this to extremes. There are some questions that do not require much thought, such as your name, job duties, etc.

It's okay to prepare for your testimony, so don't be hesitant to tell the truth if you are asked on cross examination what you did to get ready for your testimony. Arbitrators assume that advocates prepare their witnesses for the hearing. This would include going over the questions to be asked, showing them relevant documents, and preparing for cross examination. If you are asked about this, tell the truth. The arbitrator would be very surprised if you didn't do something to prepare for the hearing.

Be prepared for cross examination tactics. These include leading questions (one where the question itself suggests the answer desired), shifting subjects of inquiry, asking the same question repeatedly in a slightly different way, and demeaning or insulting questions. I continue to be amazed at how far some arbitrators will let cross examiners go past the bounds of civility and fairness, but it is a fact of life. Your advocate will brief you on the specific cross examination questions that might be asked of you.

Don't get angry. Remember, no one is going to jail after the hearing, so keep things in perspective. When you get angry, two things happen: (1) you are not thinking as you should be and may make a mistake, and (2) you lose credibility with the arbitrator. Keep your cool. I can assure you, the angrier you get, the longer you will be on the witness stand. The cross examiner will make a spectacle of you and you would have only yourself to blame because you lost your control.

If someone objects to a question asked of you, don't answer (or stop your answer) until the arbitrator has ruled on whether the question may be asked. The rules of evidence do not apply in arbitration hearings, so most questions will be allowed. Nevertheless, whether you must answer is up to the arbitrator when an objection is made. Wait for the arbitrator to rule rather than continuing your answer.

Don't answer a question about what a document says unless you have the document in front of you. Unless you are one of those few people with a photographic memory, you are likely to make a mistake in remembering exactly what a document says, when it is dated, etc. Once again, you are under oath and this is not a closed book test.

If you bring any notes or other materials to the hearing and appear to be referring to them when you testify, the other side has a right to examine them. If you need a "cheat sheet" because of memory issues, discuss it with your advocate first.

Remember, your job as a witness is to answer questions, not to ask them or make comments. A witness who tries to "turn the tables" on the questioner will quickly dig himself/herself a hole. You lose credibility with the arbitrator instantly. It's okay, of course, to ask if you don't understand a word used, want the question repeated, etc.

Beware of the meaning of common words. The examiner may ask you if something happens "a lot" or "frequently." Despite the rule above, it's okay to ask the questioner what he or she means by the word.

Remember, you may be excluded from the hearing room except during your testimony. This is common and you should not take offense. The grievant, however, has the right to be in the room the entire time as does the company representative. If, however, you are allowed to be in the room during the testimony of others, remain silent and do not interrupt the hearing or make audible sounds or gestures that could distract from the proceedings.

If you are in the hearing and something is said by another witness that you think is not right or brings up something that you want your advocate to know about, write it down on a piece of paper rather than whispering in his or her ear.

Don't be distracted by the whispered asides or gestures of the grievant during your testimony. Many grievants or union representatives will use "stage whispers" to call you a liar or something similar or roll their eyes, pretend to choke, etc. Ignore them as best you can. Be prepared to encounter this.

Be neatly groomed. This doesn't mean you have to wear a coat or tie. I tell my witnesses simply to wear what they wear to work. Discuss this with your advocate.

Don't look to your advocate as if he/she is coaching you on your answers. I see this a lot. The witness will look at his/her advocate before and after they answer the question as if looking for advice or approval. Avoid this. Look directly at your questioner.

Don't slouch in the chair. Sit up in an erect manner.

Advise your advocate if you have dietary or other medical requirements that necessitate taking periodic breaks.

Don't repeat the question before you answer it. If you do this, it looks like you are stalling for time.

Be careful what you say to your advocate or others on your side of the case during breaks. You never know when you might be overheard. Be sure your remarks will be private.

Don't talk to the arbitrator about the case during breaks or before and after the hearing. It's okay to make small talk, but keep it away from anything that is controversial. The weather is usually a safe subject.

Index

A